Scott Cohen

A Fireside Book
Published by Simon & Schuster

New York   London   Toronto   Sydney   Tokyo   Singapore

FIRESIDE
Rockefeller Center
1230 Avenue of the Americas
New York, New York 10020

FIRESIDE and colophon are registered trademarks of
Simon & Schuster Inc.

Produced by March Tenth, Inc.
Designed by Paul Leibow
Manufactured in the United States of America

10 9 8 7 6 5 4 3 2 1

Library of Congress Cataloging-in-Publication Data is available.

ISBN: 0-671-88092-6

CONTENTS

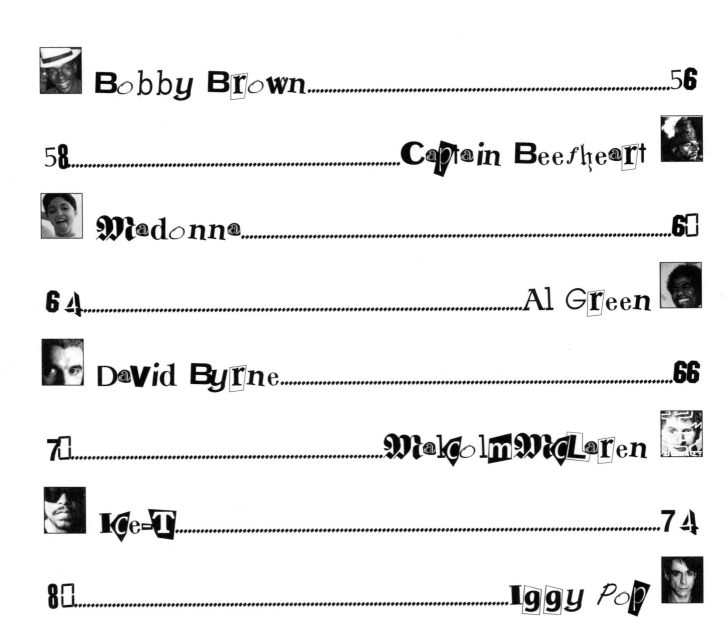

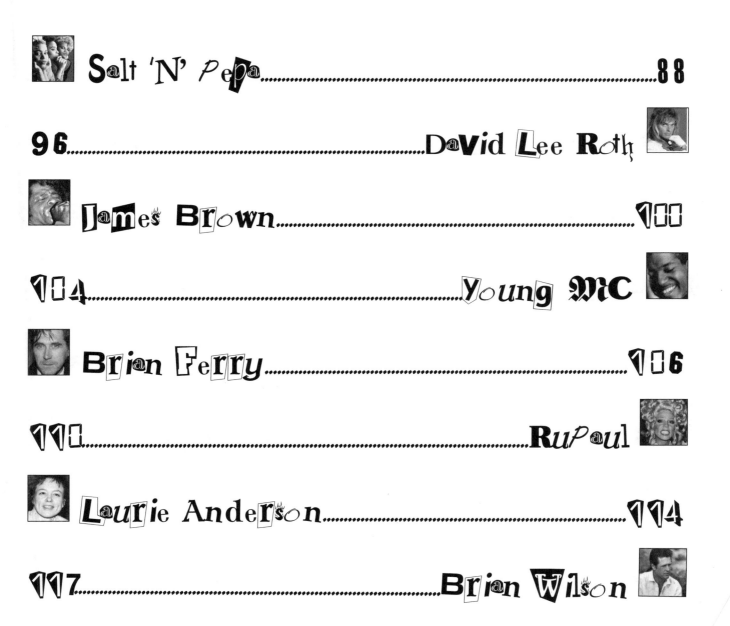

Bob dylan

A DOZEN INFLUENTIAL RECORDS
"Lady's Man," Hank Snow
"Lucille," Little Richard
"High Lonesome Sound," Roscoe Holcomb
"Tom Joad," Woodie Guthrie
"Mystery Train," Elvis Presley
"Not Fade Away," Buddy Holly
"Molly and Tenbrooks," Bill Monroe
"Get Back," Big Bill Broonzy
"Chauffeur Blues," Memphis Minnie
"Riding on Train #45," the Delmore Brothers
"Ida Red," the Smokey Mountain Boys
"Pictures From Life's Other Side," Hank Williams
"Rocky Road Blues," Gene Vincent

FIVE BANDS I WISH I HAD BEEN IN
King Oliver Band
Memphis Jug Band
Muddy Waters' Chicago Band (with Little Walter and Otis Spann)
The Country Gentlemen
Crosby, Stills & Nash

SOME MOVIES I WISH I WAS IN
The Devil and Miss Jones
I Was a Zombie for the FBI
Ben Hur
Raintree County

QUESTIONS I CAN'T ANSWER
How does it feel to be a legend?
How does it feel to have influenced a bunch of people?
What did you change your name to?
Are you somebody?
Where's your music taking you to?
Did you write that song for me?
Did you know Nixon?

11

FIVE FAVORITE MOVIE ACTRESSES
Hedy Lamarr (I can't remember what she was in, though.)
Dorothy Dandridge (I loved her in a movie she really
needed, with Trevor Howard)
Marilyn Monroe (*Asphalt Jungle*)
Jane Russell (*The Outlaw*)
Darla (Little Rascals)

THREE AUTHORS I'D READ ANYTHING BY
Tacitus
Chekhov
Tolstoy

PET PEEVES
Women who sit and eat meat all day
Salesmen who slap you on the back and wink
Preachers who preach the "wealth and prosperity"
doctrine

ONE SPORT I WISH I WAS BETTER AT
Harness racing

WHAT'S FOR DINNER
Grilled corn-on-the-cob
Black-eyed peas
Beet root salad
Spinach and pilaf
Deep-fried cauliflower
French fried chicken and gravy
French fried cabbage
Pinto beans and rice
Cocoa angel cake

EVENTS I WISH I WITNESSED
Custer's last stand
Hannibal crossing the Alps
Lindberg landing in Paris
Houdini on the East River

MY LAST SLICE OF PIZZA
Tony's, Broadway and 46th Street, 1981

A THREESOME I'D LIKE TO PLAY GOLF WITH
Paul Gauguin,
Lee Iacocca,
Edward Teller

A COUPLE OF ACTORS I'D LIKE TO PLAY ME IN MY LIFE STORY
Billy Dee Williams
Mickey Rooney

TIPS FOR GIRLS WHO'D LIKE ME TO LIKE THEM
Tell me everything.

SOMETHING I'D LIKE TO IMPROVE ABOUT MYSELF
My penmanship

SOME GREAT MINOR MASTERPIECES
"Bony Moronie"
"Surfin' Bird"
"Lonesome Town"

MY FAVORITE SHOT IN BASKETBALL
The free throw

A COUPLE OF PEOPLE I WOULDN'T MIND BEING FOR A MINUTE
Roy Acuff
Walter Matthau
Leonard Cohen

THE BEST CURE FOR THE BLUES
Ginger root

SOME PLACES I WOULDN'T WANT TO GO BACK TO
Auschwitz
Casino de Paris
Marsaille
The Horse & Hounds Tavern
Edinburgh

THINGS I'LL ALWAYS MISS
Sweet kisses from the Black Queen
Trebuki Bay at sunset
White geese in the North Carolina sky
Four angels blowing marble trumpets in Times Square

SOME THINGS I'D RATHER FORGET
Spaghetti at the airport in Helsinki
Lady Godiva at the cemetery in New Orleans
The girl with the horse's head in Mexico

MY TWO FAVORITE INGREDIENTS IN JOHNNY CAKES
Corn meal and maple syrup

HOW TO LET HER DOWN EASY
Tell her you're down and out

SOMETHING I DO EVERY DAY
Ask for forgiveness

TWO TRUTHS THAT AREN'T TRUE
God helps those who help themselves.
Actors get up at 5 A.M.

SOMETHING THEY DON'T TEACH AT SCHOOL
Satan is the ruler of this world.

THE FURTHEST THINGS FROM MY MIND
Perpetual youth
St. James' Infirmary

THE NEAREST FARAWAY PLACES
Cuba
Isle of Patmos

GAMES I PLAY
Crazy 8s
Dominoes
Chess
Hearts
Fan Tan
He Say, She Say

CLUBS I BELONG TO
Back-To-The-Wall Club
Night-Watch
Merle Haggard Fan Club
Franz Kline Fan Club
Rockin' & Rhythm Club
Backup Rider Club

ONE LAST FAVOR I'D LIKE TO ASK
"Resist not evil, but overcome evil with good."

SEVERAL THINGS STILL BLOWIN' IN THE WIND
The Three Little Pigs
The wages of sin
Lester Young's horn solo on "When Buddha Smiles"

A MYSTERY OR TWO

A lot of people from the press want to talk to me but they never do, and for some reason there's this great mystery, if that's what it is. When I think of mysteries, I don't think about myself. I think of the universe, like why does the moon rise when the sun falls? Caterpillars turn into butterflies?

DEFINITION OF COOL

Miles Davis—I loved to see him in the small clubs, playing his solo, turn his back on the crowd, put down his horn and walk off the stage, let the band keep playing, then come back and play a few notes at the end. I did that at a couple of shows; the audience thought I was sick or something.

COOL SUNGLASSES

I started out with Batman and Robin-type sunglasses. I always thought the best kind are the motorcycle helmets with the black plastic masks on them. That way, nobody can recognize the back of your head, either. What I'm looking for is a pair of glasses that can see through walls, whether they're sunglasses or not.

DEFINITION OF HOT

Lily St. Cyr (the stripper)
Dorothy Dandridge
Mary Magdalene

MY FIRST POP HERO

Johnny Ray. The last time I saw him was late '78. I think he was playing club lounges. He hadn't had a hit for a while. Maybe he needed a new record company. People forget how good he was.

SOME PEOPLE I'D LIKE TO INTERVIEW

Hank Williams,
Apollinaire,
Joseph from the Bible,
Marilyn Monroe,
John F. Kennedy,
Mohammed,
Paul the Apostle,
(maybe) John Wilkes Booth,
(maybe) Gogol,
people who died leaving a great unsolved mess behind, who left people for ages to do nothing but speculate. As far as anybody living goes, who's there to interview? Castro? Gorbachev? Reagan? The Hillside Strangler? What are they going to tell you? The destiny of the the world's wealthiest man–that doesn't interest me. I know what his reward is. Anyone who's done work that I admire, I'd rather just leave it at that. I'm not that pushy about finding out how people come up with what they come up with, so what does that leave you with? Just the daily life of somebody. You know, like "How come you don't eat fish?" That really wouldn't give me answers to what I'm wondering about.

SOMEONE WHO DIDN'T RETURN MY CALL

Walter Yetnikoff—I placed it personally, direct dial, long distance, at three o'clock in the morning.

WHAT I THINK ABOUT

I was reading a book of Nathaniel Hawthorne's letters to some girl and they were extremely private and personal. I didn't feel there was any of myself in those letters, but I could identify with what he was saying. A lot of myself crosses over into my songs. I'll write something and say to myself, I can change this, I can make this not so personal, and other times I'll say, I think I'll leave this on a personal level and if somebody wants to peek at it and make up their own minds about what kind of character I am, that's up to them. Other times I might say, well, it's too personal, I think I'll turn the corner on it, because why do I want somebody thinking about what I'm thinking about?

MY RELATIONSHIPS

Outside a song like "Positively 4th Street," which is extremely one dimensional, which I like, I don't usually purge myself by writing anything about any type of so-called relationships. I don't have the kind of relationships that are built on any kind of false pretense, not to say that I haven't. I've had just as many as anybody else, but I haven't had them in a long time. Usually everything with me and anybody is up front. My-life-is-an-open-book sort of thing. And I choose to be involved with the people I'm involved with. They don't choose me.

WHAT ATTRACTS ME TO A WOMAN

I've always been drawn to a certain kind. It's the voice more than anything. I listen to the voice first. It's that sound I heard growing up. It was calling out to me. When everything was blank and void, I would listen for hours to the Staple Singers. It's that sort of gospel singing sound. Or that voice on the Crystals' record "Then He Kissed Me"– Clydie King, Memphis Minnie, that type of thing. There's something in that voice, that whenever I hear it, I drop everything, whatever it is.

WHAT I REMEMBER ABOUT EDIE SEDGWICK

Not much. I've seen where I have read that I have had, but I don't remember Edie that well. I remember she was around, but I remember other people who, as far as I know, might have been involved with Edie. Uh, she was a great girl. An exciting girl, very enthusiastic. She was around the Andy Warhol scene, and I drifted in and out of that scene, but then I moved out of the Chelsea Hotel. We—me and my wife—lived on the third floor of the Chelsea in 1965 or '66, when our first baby was born. We moved out of that hotel maybe a year before *Chelsea Girls*, and when *Chelsea Girls* came out, it was all over for the Chelsea Hotel. You might as well have burned it down. The notoriety it had gotten from the movie pretty much destroyed it.

I think Edie was in *Chelsea Girls.* I had lost total touch with her by that time, anyway. It may just have been a time when there was just a lot of stuff happening. Ondine, Steve Paul's Scene, Cheetah. That's when I would have known Edie if I would have known her, and I did know her, but I don't recall any type of relationship. If I did have one, I think I'd remember.

MY ONLY REGRET

I once traded an Andy Warhol "Elvis Presley" painting for a sofa. I always wanted to tell Andy what a stupid thing I'd done, and if he had another painting he would give me, I'd never do it again.

MY BAR MITZVAH

There weren't too many Jews in Hibbing, Minnesota. Most of them I was related to. The town didn't have a rabbi, and it was time for me to be bar mitzvahed. Suddenly a rabbi showed up under strange circumstances, for only a year. He and his wife got off the bus in the middle of the winter. He was an old man from Brooklyn who had a white beard and wore a black hat and black clothes. They put him upstairs above the cafe, which was the local hangout.

It was a rock 'n' roll cafe where I used to hang out, too. I used to go up there every day to learn this stuff, either after school or after dinner. After studying with him an hour or so, I'd come down and boogie. The rabbi taught me what I had to learn, and after he conducted this bar mitzvah, he just disappeared. The people didn't want him. He didn't look like anybody's idea of a rabbi. He was an embarrassment. All the Jews up there had shaved their beards, and, I think, worked on Saturday. And I never saw him again. It's like he came and went like a ghost. Later I found out he was Orthodox. Jews separate themselves like that. Orthodox, Conservative, Reform, as if God calls them that. Christians, too: Baptists, Assembly of God, Methodists, Calvinists. God has no respect for a person's title. He don't care what you call yourself.

WHY I STARTED WRITING SONGS

Because things were changing all the time and a certain song needed to be written. If they had been written, I wouldn't have started to write them. But I did sing a lot of songs before I wrote any of my own. I think that's important, too.

WHAT INFLUENCED MY SONGS

I didn't start writing poetry until I was out of high school. I was eighteen or so when I discovered Ginsberg, Gary Snyder, Phillip Whalen, Frank O'Hara, and those guys. Then I started reading the French guys, Rimbaud and Francois Villion; I started putting tunes to their poems. There used to be a folk music scene and jazz clubs just about every place. The two scenes were much connected, where the poets would read to a small combo, so I was close to that for a while. My songs were influenced not so much by poetry on the page but by poetry being recited by the poets who recited poems with jazz bands.

THE FIRST EXPENSIVE THING I BOUGHT

A 1965 baby blue Mustang convertible. But a guy who worked for me rolled it down the hill in Woodstock and it smashed into a truck. I got twenty-five bucks for it.

THE NAME ON MY DRIVER'S LICENCE

Bob Dylan. It was legally changed when I went to work for Folk City a few thousand years ago. They had to get my name straight for the union.

GOING ELECTRIC

The first time I played electric before a large group of people was at the Newport Folk Festival, but I had a hit record out [*Bringing It All Back Home*], so I don't know how people expected me to do anything different. I was aware that people were fighting in the audience, but I couldn't understand it. I was a little embarrassed by the fuss, because it was for the wrong reasons. I mean, you can do some really disgusting things in life and people will let you get away with it. Then you do something that you don't think is anything more than natural and people react in that type of riotous way, but I don't pay too much attention to it.

WHEN I HEAR SOMEONE WHO SOUNDS LIKE ME

The only time it bothered me was when I was living in Phoenix, Arizona, in about '72, and the big song at the time was "Heart of Gold." I always liked Neil Young, but it bothered me every time it came on the radio. I think it was up at number one for a long time, and I'd say, "Shit, that's me. If it sounds like me it might as well be me." There I was, stuck on the desert some place, having to cool out for a while. New York was a heavy place. Woodstock was worse, people living in trees outside my house, fans trying to batter down my door, cars following me up dark mountain roads. I needed to lay back for a while, forget about things, myself included, and I'd get so far away and turn on the radio and there I am, but it's not me. It seemed somebody else had taken my thing and had run away with it, you know, and I never got over it. Maybe tomorrow.

A THING OR TWO ABOUT SOME OTHER SONGS

Of all the songs I've ever written, "Tight Connection to My Heart" might be one of the most visual. I want to make a movie out of it. I don't think it's going to be done. Of all the songs I've written, that's the one that's got characters that I can be identified with—whatever the fuck that means. I don't know. I may be trying to make it more important than it is. I don't know, maybe it should stay a song.

In most of my songs, I know who it is I'm singing about and to. Since '78, that's been true and hasn't changed. The stuff before '78,—'76, '75, '74—those people have kinda disappeared. If you see me live, you won't hear me sing too many of those songs. There's a certain area of songs, a certain period that I don't feel that close to. Like the songs on the *Desire* album, that's kind of a fog to me. But since '78, the characters have been extremely real and are still there. The ones I choose to talk about and relate to are the ones I find some kind of greatness in.

WHAT I LEARNED IN BIBLE SCHOOL

I went to Bible school at an extension of this church out in the Valley in Reseda, California. It was affiliated with the church, but I'm not a believer in that born-again type thing. Jesus told California, "A man must be born again." And Nicodemus said, "How can I go through my mother's womb?" And Jesus said, "You must be born of the spirit." And that's where that comes from, that born-again thing. People have put a heavy trip on it. People can call you what they want. The media make up a lot of these words for the definition of people. I mean, who's a person anymore? Everything's done for the media. If the media don't know about it, it's not happening. They'll take the littlest thing and make it spectacular. They're in the business of doing that. Love, truth, beauty. Conversation is a business. Spirituality is not a business, so it's going to go against the grain of people who are trying to exploit other people. God doesn't look at people and say, "That's a banker, that's a dentist, that's an oil-well driller." A lot of crooked people give a lot of money to charity. That all means nothing. If there's evil behind good, it doesn't mean the good's good. No matter how many hospitals they're building. It's all bullshit. It's called vanity of vanities. That's what the world is run on. That's how the machine turns, so if you go against that in any way, you're an outlaw. And it's tough for people to go against that. What I learned in Bible school was just another side of an extension of the same thing I believed in all along, but just couldn't verbalize or articulate. Whether you want to believe Jesus Christ is the Messiah is irrelevant, but whether you're aware of the messianic complex, that's all that's important.

THE MEANING OF THE MESSIANIC COMPLEX

All that exists is spirit, before, now, and forever more. The messianic thing has to do with this world, the flesh world, and you got to pass through this to get to that. The messianic thing has to do with the world of mankind, like it is. This world is scheduled to go for 7,000 years, 6000 years of this where man has his way, and 1,000 years when God has His way. Just like a week. Six days work, one day rest. The last thousand years is called the Messianic Age. Messiah will rule. He is, was, and will be about God, doing God's business. Drought, famine, war, murder, theft, earthquake, and all the evil things will be no more. No more disease. That's all of this world.

WHAT'S GOING TO HAPPEN

You know, when things change, people usually know, like in a revolution, people know before it happens who's coming in and who's going out. All the Somozas and Batistas will be on their way out, grabbing their stuff and whatever, but you can forget about them. They won't be going anywhere. It's the people who live under tyranny and oppression, the plain, simple people, that count, like the multitude of sheep. They'll see that God is coming. Somebody representing Him will be on the scene. Not some crackpot lawyer or politician with the mark of the beast, but somebody who makes them feel holy. People don't know how to feel holy. They don't know what it's about or what's right. They don't know what God wants of them. They'll want to know what the Messiah wants. They'll want to know what to do and how to act. Just like you want to know how to please any ruler. They don't teach that stuff like they do math, medicine, and carpentry, but now there will be a tremendous calling for it. There will be a run on godliness, just like now there's a run on refrigerators, headphones, and fishing gear. It's going to be a matter of survival. People are going to be running to find out about God, and who are they going to run to? They gonna run to the Jews, 'cause the Jews wrote the book, and you know what? The Jews ain't gonna know. They're too busy in the fur business and in the pawnshops and in sending their kids to some atheist school. They're too busy doing all that stuff to know. People who believe in the coming of the

Messiah live their lives right now as if He were here.
That's my idea of it, anyway.
I know people are going to say to themselves, "What the
fuck is this guy talking about?" but it's all there
in black and white, the written and unwritten word. I
don't have to defend this stuff. The scriptures back me up. I
didn't ask to know this stuff. It just came to me at
different times from experiences throughout my life, Other
than that, I'm just a rock 'n' roller, folk poet,
gospel-blues-protest guitar player.
Did I say that right?

SOMEONE I WAS IN ANOTHER LIFETIME

A courtesan. I would like to say I was Rimbaud or someone real cool like that, but if anyone was Rimbaud it was Dylan. I was probably some elegant female. I would like to have been Rimbaud so much, but I'm really like a woman trying to seduce him.

WHO I AM IN THIS LIFETIME

A poet. I hate to say it because poet is a sort of dumb word but in my heart I'd say I'm a writer. Or a language architect. Verlaine described Rimbaud's poetry as diamond prose. I'm a diamond prose writer.

A thief, especially when I was more boyish, looked boyish, had a boyish consciousness. To do good art you have to be a good thief. I learned this from the Rolling Stones and Dylan, because when I saw the Stones and Dylan I would come out totally drained, especially by Mick, who sucks the energy right out of you but also gives you something in return, something that inspires me to work. That's being a good thief. A bad thief deserves to get caught because he ruins it for a good thief.

I'm also a mother and a housewife.

WHAT I WAS GROOMED TO BE

A mistress. I came to New York not to be an artist but an artist's mistress. I have a completely French view of art. I used to read biographies of great people like Piaf, who really dug their men and worked for them. I was also infatuated with my father. I thought he could use a really good mistress, so I decided I would groom myself to become his mistress.

MY IDEA OF A DREAM DATE

First, my date would send me a box from Balenciaga's and in it would be the classic black dress, an orchid, and dark glasses. He would also send me black silk stockings. He would send me my whole outfit so I looked like an Italian bombshell. Then he'd call on me in a Jaguar, and if it's going to be a total dream, the Jaguar would have wings and we'd fly to the South of France. Then we'd go out for a classy dinner and there would be a menu with no prices. That to me is real class. He'd order everything. I can't stand ordering; it makes me neurotic. After that we'd go to a roulette house, like in *Band of Angels*. I'd start out the evening looking like Anouk Aimée and end up looking like Jeanne Moreau. Then he'd drive me back and kiss my hand. And we wouldn't do nothing, if you know what I mean.

WHY I WEAR BLACK AND WHITE

Blue is my favorite color but I can't wear it. I think of myself and my clothes as an extension of a movie. I love black and white movies. Ever since I saw *Don't Look Back*, I've been ruined. When I walk down the street I'm always inside a movie, all the time, so I have to dress in black and white.

THE FIRST EXPENSIVE THING I BOUGHT MYSELF

An I.D. bracelet. I know I'm scrawny looking but I don't like cheap stuff. I either like ratty stuff and have a peasant look or I look completely chic, like Audrey Hepburn in *Funny Face*. With the dough I got from a poetry reading I went straight to Tiffany's. I guess Cartier's is more classy but they didn't have anything cheap enough for me, so I went to Tiffany's, where I saw this I.D. bracelet and decided to have Rimbaud's name on it. I usually wear it on my right arm, to help me when I'm writing, and when I'm not writing I keep it on my left hand, so I can use my right hand, you know, for doing stuff at night, unless, of course, I'm sleeping alone.

THE PERFECT POEM

One that is architecturally perfect, like a pyramid. It's not like a novel—it can't have a lot of filler. It's just sitting there on the page, a universe. I have a theory I call "jewel juice," that a poem is like a gem floating in space—pure, surreal space—and that has a million facets. Or that it's a crystal, because a crystal is more alchemical.

WHAT HAPPENS WHEN I WRITE

It's a complete physical act. I pee, I sweat. If I write something sexy, I wet my pants. When people say writing isn't physical, I get pissed, because when I'm pounding my Hermes and am completely at one with my work, I just shake.

THE FURTHEST I'VE GONE FOR A LAUGH

I was caught up in the rock 'n' roll image as bad or worse than anyone. Half my friends were rock stars. A bunch of managers were thinking of doing something with me when I was in my Keith Richards stage and I was

really flashy, but you know, I'm not really a great singer, I'm not really tough, I'm not really a leather man. I'm a girl and I'm real fragile. When Janis Joplin died, I started thinking about what her problem was. We used to drink a lot together and talk about how she couldn't stand to reveal herself as being fragile. I didn't care how I revealed myself. I grew up skinny and creepy and made friends by doing Tex Ritter imitations. That's how I first became popular. I would do anything for a laugh. I'll tell you, it isn't easy for a girl who fancied herself the cosmic mistress of Modigliani to sing Tex Ritter songs.

WHAT HAPPENS WHEN A MAN FROM OUT WEST MEETS A GIRL FROM BACK EAST

The only man I've known from Out West was Sam Shepard. Out West guys think big. Sam thinks so big that he falls in love with dinosaurs, Mt. Rushmore; he thinks really big. And me, a little girl from back East, especially from New Jersey, coming from the flatlands and the swamps, thinks small. But my big dreams matched his physical looks.

WHY I CHOSE TO LOOK LIKE KEITH RICHARDS

I acted like a boy for so long that I didn't know how to act like a woman. I hadn't worn a dress for years. The only way I could learn about being a woman was from other women, so I got completely captivated by girls, which everyone took for a lesbian thing. But all I wanted to do was make myself more feminine. I liked guys so much I used to think the way to a guy's heart was by doing his homework. Now I know the way to a guy's heart is by being a woman. I even once decided to have an affair with Anita Pallenberg. That's how I got into my Keith Richards period. I thought if I looked enough like Keith Richards, Anita Pallenberg would pick up on me and maybe after we were done messing around, Keith and I could mess around. But these fantasies were completely intellectual and had nothing to do with my body. I didn't even know a woman could masturbate.

They fucked for two days in thunder and lightning
and the sky was just like totally opening up,
the fields were on fire, the whole world was going berserk.
There was radical strife and poverty and people
killing each other and everything was in flames and they
were fucking right through it. Then he says at the
end,"I'll be leavin' tomorrow." He's an Italian and he's
not accepted in this French village. He's so stupid.
You don't tell a woman you're leaving her after you fuck
her for two days. If you are, you split fast,
because you're gonna die. So she walks into town, like
she's a chaste school teacher with a bun and
everything, all fucked up. She's like a lioness and she
comes in with her chiffon dress all bloody and filthy and
the women all get hysterical. She's like the symbol
of purity, their Madonna, Marianne Faithful, and they
cannot believe she's been so defiled. "Was it the Italian?
Was it, was it?" She looks at them and she goes, "Oui."
She says "oui" so great, it's like, "yeah." In fact, I coulda
sworn she said "yeah." They kill the guy with
sledge hammers, pitch forks and stuff, but that's another
story. Thing was, after she sold him up the river,
she was just exhausted from being fucked so great in the
rain and lightning.

A PLACE CALLED HEAVEN

Everyone thinks there's one heaven. Mohammed
personally mapped out seven. If he got to seven, you know
there's more. Christianity made us think there's one
heaven and Jesus might be top dog there, but there's other
heavens. Mohammed saw Jesus and he went further up,
and there's people past him. Kids today pass him. Jesus is
small time. He's of the flesh. Like a rock star—
you can fuck him.

SOMETHING SACRED

Dope. I never took drugs in the '60's. I read Anais Nin's
Collage in high school and it had a whole passage about
acid. I thought this is really something magical, it must be
for artists. You would have to really have earned it,
to take this drug. And all of a sudden it was out in the
streets. Any asshole could buy it.
In high school I was always like a backwards rebel. I
rebelled against my friends. My friends sniffed glue and
drank Tiger Rose and said you got to do it to be cool and I
said I don't have to burn my brains out

and turn into a human airplane at the age of fifteen. Mind
expansion's really great when your mind is
expanded. Instead of burning out the baby cells, you
would extend the ones that are experienced because then
you can go on forever.

MY HEAVIEST EXPERIENCE
Merging with God

HOW I BECAME AN ART ADDICT

Art protected me for a while. I didn't need no drugs. My
vice was art. I'd get a Kodak and go to the Museum
of Modern Art to see the DeKooning Retrospect and take
hundreds of black and white pictures of Woman I; her
hands, her feet, her hairdo. It was like I really shot her. I
did drawings inspired by her. I did drawings of my poems.
They're like illuminated manuscripts:
angels fucking, angels ripping out each other's guts.
Angels are great because they are beyond gender. When
you think of angels you don't think of boy or girl.
You think of light. And I just figured for drugs, you really
had to be an angel. I figured you really had to
earn the right to have drugs. I feel like I earned it. I got
three boxes. I got my grass box, my hash box, and
my opium box. There's a quote in this book: "In the
morning they smoke, in the afternoon they smoke, in the
evening they smoke. In truth, they smoke all day." It's like
I was born stoned. Drugs to me are a ritual. Man needs
rituals. The nice thing about the peace pipe or the
joint is the ritual of it. All through time this ritual has
existed. I think I earned the rite. I like smoking pot.
Actually, I would be just as happy smoking Kools. Look at
Jeanne Moreau smoking a cigarette—she is so high. For me
drugs are for work. Pleasure is private. There's pleasure
within work, but private pleasure is like when you're in
love with someone.

AN EARLY PREMONITION

I have '50s Vogues with early pan shots, pale roses, and
models with necks that went on forever. I have ones with
Scavullo, when he used to shoot little kids—little girls with
big hats and white stockings like in Alice in Wonderland.
And architecture, like Jean Shrimpton with a space helmet,
Edie Sedgwick with the blonde hair and the dark
eyebrows—like she didn't mess around. Platinum hair
and black brows. She was really something. I saw her and

SOME THINGS I NEED TO LEARN
More finesse
Grammar
To walk correctly
To wear heels
To sit correctly in a taxi

A TYPICAL MYSTICAL EXPERIENCE
I'm laying on the bed and there's a black string laying on the floor. All of a sudden the black string turns into a black praying mantis. It gets up on its haunches and stands six feet tall. It has a skin tight black satin gown on that goes to the floor. It's feelers are made of black satin. It has a mantle made of diamonds and it is singing a torch song, a torch solo in some passionate nightclub. Then waltz music comes on and the praying mantis starts to waltz in time. There is a crystal chandelier hanging above its head and the crystal lights from the chandelier start to mix with the light from the diamonds and when I look into the refractions I see dancers in a huge ballroom with polished floors. The dancers are spinning and spinning like in *Little Black Sambo* when the tiger spun to butter. They spin until they form a huge diamond and the diamond spins until all its facets are smooth and it is like a crystal ball and for one second, just one second, I pluck it out of the air.

A RULE I TRY TO LIVE BY
Always wash my own sheets. I won't let anyone else wash the sheets that me and the one I love sleep on

SOMEONE WHO'S REALLY GREAT
Jeanne Moreau. She's so great, the way she conquers a guy. She's so self-contained. She could start a forest fire. There's this scene where superficially she's like a chaste school teacher but inside she's like barbed wire. There's this burly Italian Burt Lancaster, his shirt open, a big gold St. Christopher medal on his chest, who walks through the fields. He's reeking of the wine fields and he's got a chainsaw because he's a lumberjack and there's all this tension because you know they're gonna do it and when they do, they don't let you down.It's so heavy. They fuck in the field. He rips off her dress and she's like an instant animal. He makes her crawl through the field barking like a dog and she's got this chiffon dress on, which he rips to shreds.

Andy Warhol in the Philadelphia Museum of Art. It was like seeing a black and white movie in person. She really got me. It was something weird. I really think you know your future, if you want to. Like there I was, I had really bad skin, I was really skinny and really fucked up but I never knew I was going to do work for *Vogue*. I didn't know how, but I just knew it.

THE TROUBLE WITH AMERICANS

Americans just don't know what being a movie star's all about. That's the whole thing to me—movies. I used to think it was being a model. I modeled at the Museum School. I modeled for Robert Mapplethorpe. In fact, when I go to work and stuff, where it says "profession," I always put "artist's model." Once I wrote "rock 'n' roll star" just for the hell of it.

I'd like to model for DeKooning. I know how to get to DeKooning. It's easy. I met DeKooning once in a bar and he put his hand on my knee right away. I knew I could model for him.

I was so fucked up-looking in school, but it just didn't matter. Besides an artist, I wanted to be a movie star. I don't mean an American movie star. I mean like Anouk Aimée in *La Dolce Vita*. I couldn't believe her in those dark glasses and that black dress and that sports car. I thought that was the heaviest thing I ever saw. Anouk Ainee with that black eye. It made me always want to have a black eye—forever. It made me want to get a guy to knock me around so I'd always look great.

MOST UNFORGETTABLE BED I'VE SLEPT IN

When I went to Paris I stayed at this hotel called the Hotel of Strangers, in the attic room where Charles Cros and Rimbaud lived. The guy says nobody rents this room because it's the attic room and from reading the biographies, I know it's the room where he stayed with Charles Cros. I said I will pay anything, just let me stay up there. It was so dirty. It was like in the movies when they go into the haunted house and they'd hit everything and there'd be tons of dust and spiders and the bed was shaped like bodies. In fact, I'm sure it was in the same bed because they said no one had been in that room in like years. It was a tiny bed on a metal ramp. You could see the bodies where the people slept. It was the bed where Charley and Rimbaud slept.

A PICTURE THAT SUMS ME UP BEST
A cup of coffee (Java), a pack of cigarettes (Kools), and a pair of dark glasses, like Dylan wore (*Don't Look Back*).

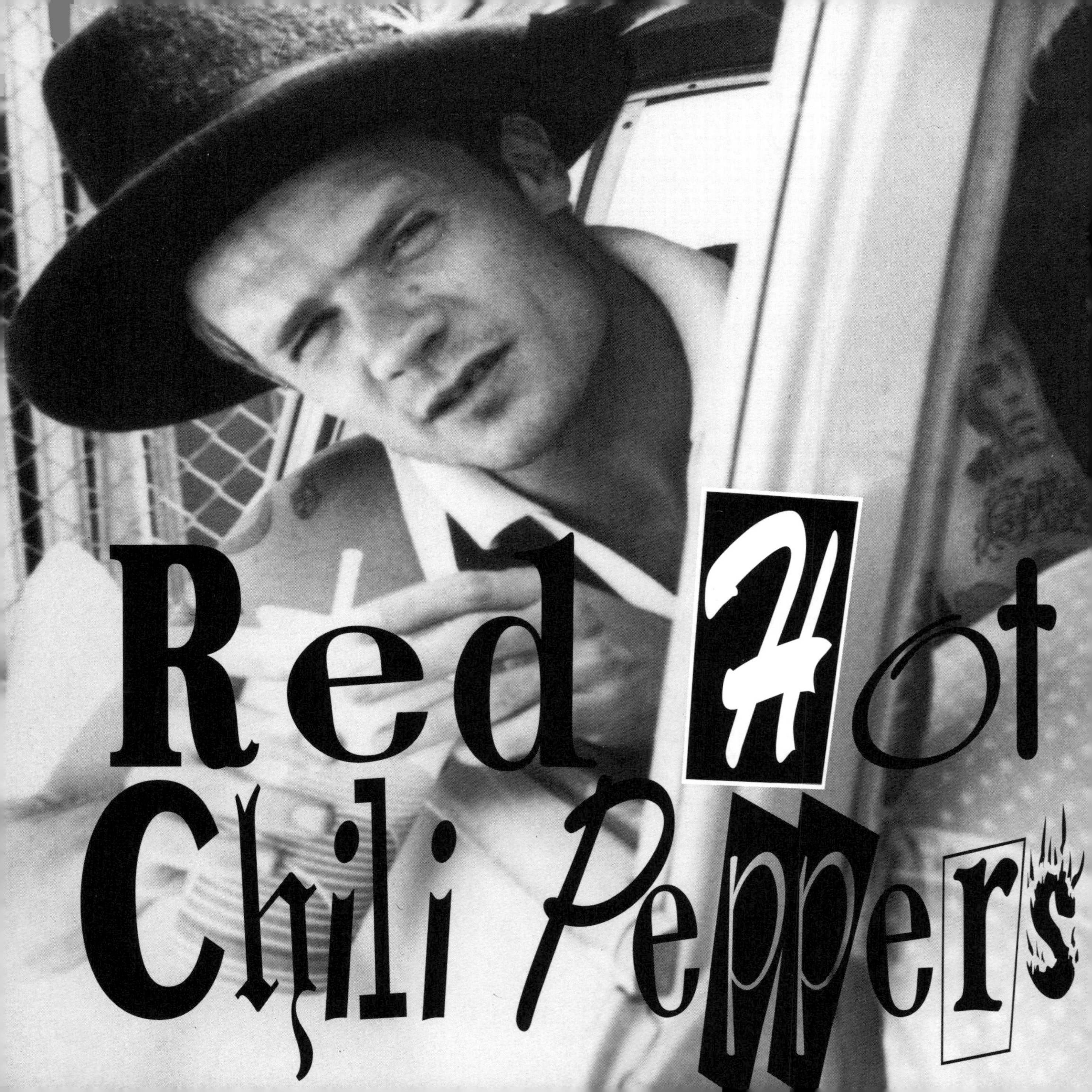
Red Hot
Chili Peppers

BANDS WE WISH WE COULD PLAY IN
The Jimi Hendrix Experience
Germs
Louis Armstrong Hot Five
Billie Holiday's band with Lester Young
Led Zep
P-Funk
The Skidmore Stravinski Orchestra of 1982 while on a European tour. Although none of these
bands match the raw power, emotional release, or the hardcore passion of Milli Vanilli.

HOW THE CHILI PEPPERS GOT STARTED
Flea:
I grew up in a jazz household and wanted to be a
trumpeter. When I got older I got into punk and that kind of energy. When I picked up the bass,
it came out as funk. One night, a friend of ours who was one of the more interesting freaks in Hollywood
was doing a crazy cabaret-music costume-dance thing, and as a joke, Anthony, Hillel Slovak,
Jack Irons, and myself got together on openinging night.
Anthony had just seen Grandmaster Flash and was
translating poems he had written into rap songs, and I could play some funky grooves. We performed
one song, "Out in L.A.," which we had never rehearsed; it was a natural explosion of funk and wildness.
The next thing we knew, there were lines around the block and record companies on the phone.

BIGGEST INFLUENCES
Magic Johnson
Traci Lords, the greatest porno star the world has ever known, who can make one breast go clockwise and the other counter clockwise simultaneously. Her orgasms are so incredibly musical that we had to include one of them in the guitar solo on the song "Stone Cold Bush."

DEFINITION OF HOT
Thomas Dolby's anal cavity after he's eaten Mexican food with George Clinton

THE MOST TOUCHING EXPERIENCE WE'VE HAD AS A GROUP
When this unknown Las Vegas stripper bent over in front of us at the strip counter, plucked a single pubic hair, and blew it toward us like a kiss.

FRUIT WE MOST IDENTIFY WITH
Bananas. We'd love to have a little oval sticker of our faces appearing on every one.

MY FIRST PUBLIC EXPOSURE
Flea:
The evening we climbed the billboard on the corner of Westwood and Wilshire Boulevard, supposedly one of the biggest intersections in the country, and wagged the weenies at the world

HOW I MET ANTHONY
Flea:
In high school, when we were both about fifteen. I had someone in a headlock when Anthony came by and told me to let him go. This was in 1977 when everybody at school had long hair and was into Led Zeppelin—except Anthony, this new kind from Michigan. He had a flat top and looked like a pit bull. I let go of the kid. After, we became friends and went skiing. We took a Greyhound up to Mammoth Mountain and slept in the laundry room of a condo. To keep warm we put quarters in the dryer.

SOMETHING ELSE WE LIKE TO DO TOGETHER
Anthony:
Jump off the roofs of apartment buildings into the swimming pools below. (Once I got overconfident and missed. I got a compression fracture of my lumbar-three vertebrae. It's been bothering me lately, so I'm seeing a twelfth-generation Chinese acupuncturist.
(Once I went to a 78-year-old dentist in Memphis to have a tooth pulled, and when the dentist walked in hunched over and shaking, I felt very nervous. When the dentist found out I was in a band, he got chatty. He said he used to do Elvis's teeth. Then he went into the back room and returned with Elvis's bridgework.)

TV SITCOM WE'D MOST LIKE TO GUEST STAR ON
"The Bill Cosby Show," as the adopted sons of the Huxtable family

TIPS FOR GIRLS WHO WANT US TO LIKE THEM
Treat us like dogs.
Ignore us.
Turn your noses up at us, and if we ask to call you, say, "Oh, I'm not feeling very callish."

THE LAST GIRLS IN THE WORLD WE WOULD WANT TO BE
The Bangles

SOMETHING MONEY CAN'T BUY
Anthony:
My tattoos. The richest person in the world couldn't buy them. He'd have to sit there and pay for them in pain. It feels like you're giving birth to a small hippopotamus.

FAVORITE FORMS OF TORTURE
The old glass tube up the penal shaft, shattered to bits
Having to look at Milli Vanilli's ugly anus faces

A MISCONCEPTION ABOUT THE CHILI PEPPERS
We're not really obsessed with our penises, though exact reproductions cast in gold can be seen hanging from the neck of L.L. Cool J in his upcoming video.

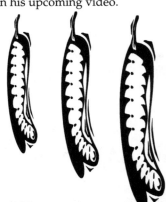

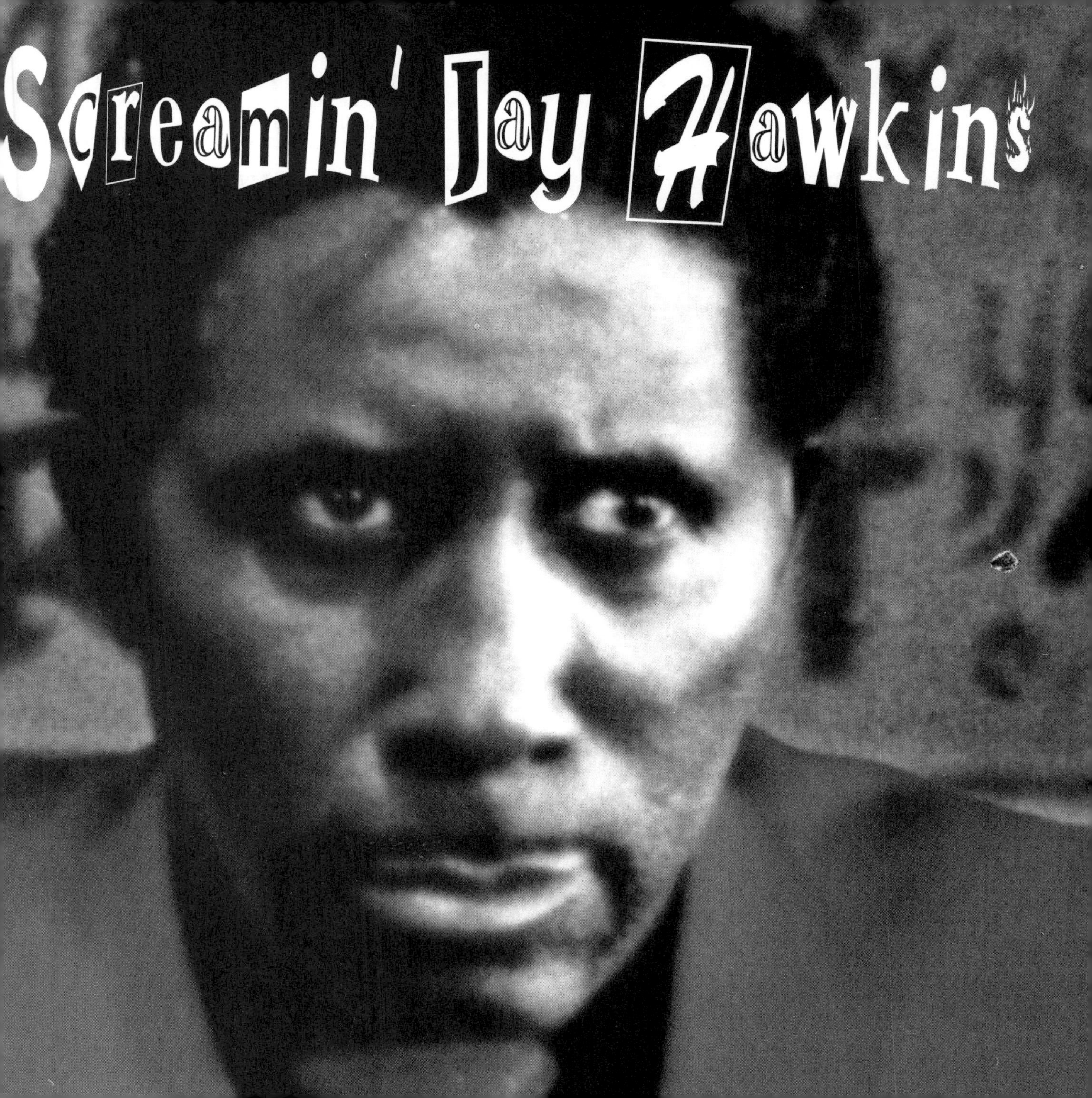
Screamin' Jay Hawkins

A FEW INFLUENTIAL RECORDS
"Ol' Man River"
"Summertime"
"My Mother's Eyes," by Paul Robeson, whom I liked
because he was a rebel who fought the system in the
United States during the '20s and the '30s, went to Russia,
and made motion pictures there because he didn't
get too much work here and refused to be an Uncle Tom
like Stepin' Fetchit, Eddie Rochester Anderson,
Lena Horn, Ethel Waters, or Buckwheat
"Caldonia," by Louie Jordan
"Shake A Hand," by Faye Adams
"After Hours," by Erskine Hawkins
"Long Gone," by Sonny Thompson,
anything by
Tiny Bradshaw, Arnette Cobb, Amos Milburn,
Gene Ammons, Sonny Stitt, Charlie Parker,
Coleman Hawkins, Shirley and Lee, Nat King Cole,
Charles Brown, the Ink Spots, the Mills Brothers,
Tiny Grimes, and Fats Domino,
even though he is conceited, self-centered, and
an asshole on top of that

WHY I'M CALLED SCREAMIN'
I didn't think I could sing like Nat King Cole, so I decided
to scream. Nobody else was doing it. James Brown is the
world's greatest howler, but he can't scream. I can scream
in tune, in any key.

THINGS THAT MAKE ME SCREAM
Being black
Prejudice
Marrying a girl who said she was pregnant after I'd just
spent two years in Alaska and was too foolish to
know better

WHAT I'D WEAR TO HAVE MY PORTRAIT PAINTED
A black suit with yellow polka dots and green stripes over
that with a purple scarf around my neck, white ruffles on
my sleeves, pants with white pleats on each side above
white shoes, a snake around my neck, and
a bone in my nose

THE TRUE KING OF ROCK 'N' ROLL
Diana Washington, as nasty as she was

SOMETHING I WANTED TO DO BUT NEVER DID
Sing opera. Again, that goes back to Paul Robeson, but
when I got into the business, opera didn't get into the
charts; they were just putting rhythm and blues out.

THE DEFINITION OF THE BLUES
Being hungry, being evicted, your wife leaving you for
another man, and your children calling him "daddy."

SOME THINGS THAT AREN'T TRUE
The white people don't have the blues.
Bill Haley had the blues and so did Carl Perkins
and Elvis Presley.

the white man is superior and the black man stinks.
I've never seen a Black armpit in a deodorant commercial
on TV, only a white armpit.

The Statue of Liberty is in New York.
It's within the waters of the New Jersey shoreline.

Sam Cooke was killed by a motel clerk who thought he
was going to rob her. Sam Cooke was killed by the Mafia.
All he did was chase a woman, while still in his shorts,
because she stole his wallet, and when he ran into the office
after her, this black woman shot him. It was a setup. Sam
Cooke fought the establishment. He was making too much
money, and when a black man gets that big, there's got to
be a white man behind him, and Sam didn't want a
white manager.

THREE WHITE PEOPLE WHO'VE SPURRED ME ON
Alan Freed, who put the coffin in my act

Louis Dulfon, who gave me my own license to run my
booking agency here in California, which
is called Hawkshaw Talent Company

Jim Jarmusch, who came out with *Stranger Than Paradise*
and used "I Put a Spell on You" in it and put me in his
movie *Mystery Train*

THE FIRST EXPENSIVE THING I BOUGHT
A hearse with zebra wall tires, instead of white wall tires,
to carry the coffin that Alan Freed put in my act.

forced her to get on a bus and go to Cleveland. That bus arrived in Cleveland just in time for her to have me and drop me at the nearest welfare center. Then she talked a tribe of Blackfoot Indians who were very wealthy into taking me out of that welfare home when I was eighteen months old and raising me. I learned all about roots from living in the forest without no blanket and no food. I learned how to eat certain bark, plants, and flowers, how to get certain stones out of ponds and rivers and make rock soup and how to cure pains and cuts with certain plants—strictly old home remedies. If my Blackfoot Indian mother was from Africa, you would call her a witch doctor; if she was from New Orleans, you'd call her a voodoo priestess. I just put it to music.

THE NEAREST FARAWAY PLACE

San Fernando Valley, where I bought a home in a section where people are quiet, mind their own business, and there are no drug addicts. Unfortunately, I'm always being bothered by door-to-door salesmen.

THE TRUEST WORDS EVER SAID

"People change, but never according to plan."

"Look for the worst, hope for the best, and accept whatever happens."

"It takes ass to get ass." I went through two wars and I'm still here. I got more marks on my body than the average crossword puzzle from knives, bombs, bullets, and being cut in half by a Japanese colonel in a prisoner of war camp.

MY FAMILY HISTORY

There were seven of us with one mother and different daddies. My sister once told me that as long as my mother didn't mess with no black people, she had it made. She had babies by a Chinese man and a baby by a white man. My father was from Arabia. My mother traveled, just like Paul Robeson. She had a lot of money that was inherited. There's a bunch of Hawkinses in Washington, D.C., who are filthy rich; I have no idea how they made their money. I understand when my mother was pregnant with me in Washington, D.C., they stoned, beat, and kicked her and

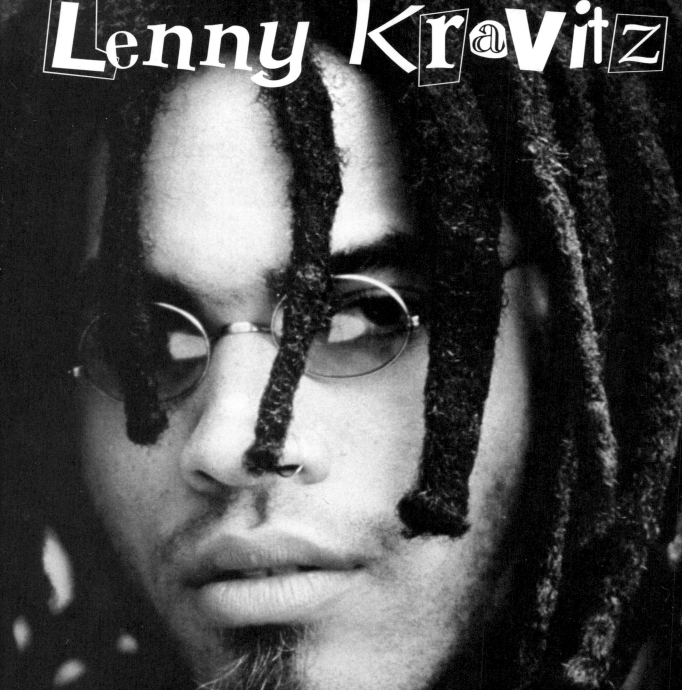

HOW I BECAME A HIPPIE

It's not that I'm fascinated with the sixties. In fact, I don't feel anything for the sixties. Because of the clothes I wear and because I sang about love and peace, people made me out to be more of a sixties thing than I really intended to be or am. I had no thought about the sixties when I made *Let Love Rule*. I just wanted to make music with real instruments. It was also the beginning of my consciousness about the planet and how we're fucking it up. So I sang about that too and all of a sudden I was King Sixties. It's not like I have lava lamps in my house.

WHAT IS IN MY HOUSE

An opium bed
Pillows everywhere
Wild fabrics
A big piece of silk that's like a parachute hanging
from my ceiling
Beads hanging from the doorways—My place is more
Turkish whorehouse-opium den.

WHAT I REMEMBER MOST ABOUT THE SIXTIES

Besides the records—being four years old in 1968 and my parents dragging me around to some cultural affair, whether it be poetry in the park or Shakespeare in the park or a classical concert in the park or Bobby Short at the Carlyle. New York was much more free back then. I lived on Fifth Avenue and 82nd Street, the best place you could possibly live, right across the street from the Metropolitan Museum of Art. Central Park was my backyard.

A FEW THINGS ABOUT MY PARENTS

I was closer to my mom, not because she was black, but because she was really cool. My dad was very strict; he had been an army sergeant in Korea. Obviously he must have been hip to marry a black woman back then. Especially to be Jewish and marry a black woman in 1963.

My mother's side didn't care that he was white. They were more concerned that he was married once before and it didn't work. They wanted to make sure he'd take care of their daughter.

My grandparents lived in Bedford-Stuyvesant and I spent the weekends there. I really looked forward to going. I could be a bit more raggedy. The people were as poor as fuck and I knew things were different from Fifth Avenue because they were drinking out of jelly and peanut butter jars instead of glasses and sitting on milk crates around the kitchen table, but whatever they had, they'd share it with you.

HOW MY MOTHER ENDED UP ON TELEVISION

She was invited to audition. She went away to do the pilot and thought she'd be back in six weeks. It went on for twelve years. She played the black woman married to the white guy. When they were considering her for the role, Norman Lear walked up to her and said, "I hope you don't take offense to this, but your husband in the show is going to be white. I don't know if this is going to make you feel uncomfortable." She pulled out her wallet and said, "This is my husband." At school, everyone thought her TV husband was my father. Coincidentally, my ex-wife [Lisa Bonet] is also half-Jewish and half-black. She had the same experiences as I did, except her father's black and her mother's white.

WHAT IT'S LIKE BEING HALF-BLACK, HALF-WHITE

When I see a Woody Allen movie, I'm howling in the aisles because I have family like that. And I can go to a Spike Lee movie and I know that scene well. I've lived them both. I was very white when I was born and had really straight hair. I didn't get brown until I was three or four. My mom used to dress like a fox and when she took me grocery shopping, the nannies would say, "My God, your boss treats you well to dress you in those fancy clothes." They thought she was the nanny of this little white child.

THE TOUGHEST THING ABOUT BEING A BLACK JEW

Wearing a yarmulka with an Afro. I had to pin it on. I went to Hebrew school, but I couldn't handle everybody staring at me like I was Michael Jackson.

FIRST POP STAR SEX SYMBOL

Batgirl. I remember lusting after her when she was on TV.

up. I know every Kiss song on the guitar. My room was covered in posters. On Halloween I went to school dressed up in leotards, chains, big boots, and Gene Simmons makeup.

WHAT MY FRIENDS THOUGHT ABOUT THAT

My Black friends did not get it at all. And my White friends thought Kiss was most uncool. They were into Led Zeppelin. By then we lived in L.A. and I was a very good skateboarder. We'd jump over people's backyard fences when they were out of town and skate in their drained swimming pools. Kiss music and skateboards; I have a weird background. At the same time I'd go see Bobby Short; I've known him since I was three. And I'd see Duke Ellington perform at the Rainbow Room. I even sat on his lap. The guy who took me away from Kiss was Prince. Hardcore Prince. *Prince for You* and *Dirty Mind.* He was doing what nobody else Black was doing, wearing panties and trench coats and had his hair all processed and wild. I wanted to be Prince.

Then I got into Bowie and wanted to be David Bowie. Then I got into being Romeo Blue. When you're fifteen and want to play music and you want to be this cool thing, you don't want to be called Lenny Kravitz. Then I got tired of being other people and became Lenny Kravitz.

CHILDHOOD IDOLS

Michael Jackson. When I was eight, nine, ten, I wanted to be Michael Jackson. Not Michael Jackson that we know now. The real Michael Jackson with the big fucking nose, the black skin and the kinky Afro. My mom bought me those clothes—vests and suede and fringe and shirts with big puffy sleeves.

Jimi Hendrix. He had it all: the music, the pimp attitude, the big dick.

Kiss. When I was thirteen, fourteen, fifteen, I was a major Kiss fan. Something about that makeup, the music, and them being larger-than-life creatures and you didn't know who they were fucked me

DaVid Bowie

MY FIRST POP HERO

Little Richard, singing "She's Got It" in 1956, when I was nine years old. It was absolute magic. I couldn't believe anybody could make that sound. I immediately sent away for a glossy of Little Richard with his big pompadour, eye makeup, and shiny suit, playing away on the piano, with the saxophones in the background. I knew I could never be Little Richard, but I could be one of his sax players, so I got my father to loan me the money to buy a saxophone. Not long ago I had dinner with Little Richard for the first time and I was absolutely stunned to see my idol has the same eye problem as me. Little Richard and I have the same eyes!

HOW I GOT MY EYE

George Underwood punched me in it. It was over this
girl. It was my fault. I knew he was going out
with her and I decided I wanted to go out with her as
well. Then he came at me with a lunch punch. I was
shocked that anyone could be that angry.

WHEN I DECIDED TO BE A POP STAR

I knew I could never be Little Richard, but I could be one
of his sax players, so I got my father to loan me the money
to buy a saxophone. It was a Selmer, made of
some strange Bakelite kind of material. Creamy plastic
with all the gold keys on it.

A COUPLE OF OTHER EARLY INFLUENCES

John Rechy's *City of Night*
The Queen—a documentary film on drag queens

WHERE MY AMBITION AND DRIVE CAME FROM

Wanting to escape myself

MY FIRST POP FASHION HEROS

The Mods. They made their first of two or three outings
in England in 1960-61, when I was thirteen or fourteen.
They wore Italian suits, short boxy jackets,
tight white linen trousers tapered to fourteen inches, and
Chelsea boots with florescent pink or green socks
and eye shadow that matched the socks.

Syd Barrett. The first person in rock I had seen with
makeup on; black nail polish, lots of mascara, black eye
shadow. There was something so otherworldly about him.
Of course we found out later he had mental problems.

THE BEST AND WORST YEARS OF MY LIFE

Artistically, 1977-81 were absolutely dynamic. I was
discovering things about myself as a musician. There was
a lot more freedom in me than I realized. I was
allowed to lower my musical differences because of my
collaboration with Brian Eno. He's the Guardian
of Hip. He treats studios the way no other person has. He
works with it like an instrument, which is
actually quite the thing now, especially in dance music,
but at that particular time, there was no one else
doing that, except for a couple of Germans. He really
hipped me to the potential of arranging musical accidents.

That whole period with him was a joy ride that concluded with *Scary Monsters.* Then began the "Let's Dance" thing, which covered three albums, *Let's Dance, Tonight,* and *Never Let Me Down,* where I thought I was almost treading water. Not *Let's Dance*; that was a rediscovery of the White-English ex-art-student-meets-Black-American funk, so it was a refocusing of *Young Americans.* But the two after that had bunches of songs that I mistreated. I didn't really apply myself. I wasn't quite sure what I was supposed to be doing. I wish there was someone around who could have told me.

WHY I AVOIDED ROMANTIC RELATIONSHIPS
I was scared shitless that it would turn out like my mother and father.

MOST PAINFUL ALBUM
Low. There's oodles of pain on that album. That was my first attempt to kick cocaine. And I moved to Berlin to do it. I moved out of the coke capital of the world into the smack capital of the world. Thankfully I didn't have a feeling for smack, so it wasn't a threat. In fact, I found the city itself to be wonderful. It's never been the same since they took the wall down.

SOMETHING I COULDN'T SAY BEFORE BUT I CAN NOW
I think I was always one-sided. I was somebody who battled very arduously to block out his emotions so nobody could ever get in. I was cut off from my feelings since I was maybe four years old. It's not until you start redressing your life, or reevaluating it, that you become aware that that's what you've been for many, many years. I blocked all my emotions on all levels to the point where, until 1988, I didn't even know how I felt.

WHERE ZIGGY STARDUST AND THOSE OTHER CHARACTERS CAME FROM
Obviously, on a psychological basis, they sprung from a deep need to protect myself. I just picked up the zeitgeist of what was happening, the general feeling that was in the air. It was like doing a painting. The characters just happened to be right for that period. They represented something that was happening socially, either wittingly or subconsciously. I'm not a good finger wagger. I'm not a good moralist. What I'm much better at

doing is conjuring up atmospheres that the audience will recognize and associate with. Not necessarily on a narrative level, but definitely to feel it as a description of their pain and hopefully some of their joy. As far as I'm concerned, I dropped characters after the Thin White Duke, in 1976. Everything I've done subsequently on stage was as near as you can get to a guy who was just presenting his songs. The suits might have been interesting and the staging was interesting, but there was no character. It was as much as I could conceivably do to present myself as a singer.

A MAJOR FLAW IN MY CHARACTER
I try to control people.

IF I WERE A LADY
I was already Lady Stardust. I think that will do.

WHAT BECAME OF ALL MY OLD COSTUMES
I've kept everything I've ever worn since 1971. I have the original pair of platform shoes—the first to appear in the west—designed by Kansai; they're up in the attic of a house. I have all of Ziggy's clothes. Everything. I had to get rid of some of my street clothes, because it was taking up space. Most of it I signed and gave to auction. Both I and Eno—because he has some extraordinary clothes that he used to wear in Roxy Music—were asked to put our stuff in the Victoria and Albert Museum in London. I was quite willing to loan them but they said you have to give them. Give them? No way. Too many tears went into them to give them away.

HOW TO LIVE
A day at a time. That serves me very well. I think it's the greatest principle of all. When I first heard that phrase, I couldn't believe how close it was to the Buddhist principles. There was a Zen master who called the Twelve Step Program the Dharma of the West. Dealing with my life is not a task to be completed, it's a process. I was always thinking I got to get this done and then everything will be okay.

HOW MY LFE HAS CHANGED

In the past I cared a lot more about what people think. I stopped caring in the mid-70s, when I realized no matter what I said or did, people were going to interpret it in their own way, but I didn't replace it with anything helpful. Finally, by the end of the 1980s, I started to care about how I think about things, and that's been the big change.

THE PRICE OF FAME

The only thing I ever got out of fame was a better table in a restaurant. And for that I gave up being able to relate to people. I was so painfully aware that people would approach me differently than they would the next guy. It was always a joy to go some place where I'd met someone who had absolutely no conception of what I do.

MY DEFINITION OF COOL

Paul Smith. He's a great British designer, but I also like his attitude about himself. He's very modest and full of grace. There's something clunky about English fashion that I like. It's not as svelte as the Italians. Only the English can wear it well.

I used to think Armani was terribly unhip, but now I think he's very hip.

Jack Kerouac was terribly cool; the younger William Burroughs—he's worth a night. And Bryan Gysin—there's a man who's ultra cool. He was such an inspiration to so many. And he was so at ease with himself, so at ease with the idea that life is terminal. When I was younger I thought Jack Bruce was very cool.

Miles Davis tried too hard to be cool; I guess he was over cool. That starts to become gawky; it starts you thinking that maybe the person isn't playing with a full deck. I'm not sure insanity's cool anymore.

I used to think insanity was it. If I made any deals in my life, it was with insanity. Now I think it's just potty.

JUST TO SET THE RECORD STRAIGHT

I never much cared for my legs. In my race of people, the heavier legs were more stylish and mine were always long and thin—very thin, right up to the middle thigh.

My legs are kind of funny. From a certain angle, the lower legs look even stronger than the upper legs. So when people said I had great legs, I didn't put much value on it. Later on in life I realized there are places in the world where long legs dominate fashion, so finally I got around to appreciating them.

HOW I CARE FOR MY LEGS

I don't. Basically, I'll do a shave when I'm bathing. If I feel good enough, I'll do a wax.

WHY I'M NOT A L'EGGS GIRL

Because they don't come in colors for black people. We really have to stay in the bronze tones, otherwise it comes up ash.

SHOES I WEAR

I was doing Maude Frizon for a long time, then I went on to Azzadine—on one tour I wore Azzadine boots, which weren't good for my leg line, but I wore them anyway because they were rock 'n' roll. And I'm doing a bit of Manolo Blahnik, privately. I'm also into Robert Clergerie, who makes great lace-ups, which I wear with Armani suits. They got an order on hold for me, so whenever I want a shoe in whatever color, they can make it. I wear size 8 1/2 A or B.

SHOES I OWN

I designed my closet when I was living in Sherman Oaks
and I had wooden shoe racks anchored to the
walls, so my shoes wouldn't be on the floor, and I
counted nearly two hundred pairs,
which I've since narrowed down to one hundred.

FAVORITE DESIGNERS

I started, way back in the days of the minidress, with Louie
Azzaro chain things. Now it's always Azzadine Alaia for
my stage wear, and if he doesn't get a line out quick
enough, then I'll just get ready-to-wear or have someone
just make up something.

HOTTEST SONG IN MY REPERTOIRE

"Better Be Good To Me" or "Respect"

HOW I KEEP MY WIG ON DURING THOSE SONGS

It's clipped onto my hair, which I wear in braids.

WHY I WEAR WIGS

I was brought up with Indian people and church people.
There was a little bit of radio, very little makeup, and no
wigs. So when I started to sing I was using my
own hair and the image was good. Then I overbleached my
hair and heavily damaged it and I had to wear wigs
because a physician said the only way my damaged hair
would grow back was to cut it off. I was really embarassed,
but the people went nuts. Of course, I started to
like the long hair. That was in 1962 and I never stopped
wearing wigs. But I never have more than three
at a time. I don't wear them off the rack. I make
my own. I've worn hair from all over the world. The
person who works for Bob Mackie makes them and
I basically remake them to my own taste.

THE LIFE SPAN OF A WIG

Stage wigs—about a year; private wigs—about two years.
On stage I don't wear the very soft, curly hair.
I wear the more coarse because there's quick changes and a
lot brushing and you lose a lot of hair.

ONE TIME I WASN'T WEARING A WIG

When I left Ike. My head was too swollen to wear it. I just
put a cape on over my bloody clothes, tied a stretch wrap
around my head, and put on a pair of sunglasses.

THINGS IKE'S BEATEN ME WITH

A metal shoe stretcher, shoes, phones, wire hangers, fists, walking canes. Once he threw boiling coffee in my face. He gave me black eyes and swollen lips. He broke my arm and my ribs and busted my jaw (but never once did he sit on a wig).

HOW I REFER TO MYSELF WHEN I'M BY MYSELF

My real name was Anna Mae, way back in Tennessee and grade school. Then I went north and changed my name to Ann in high school, but now it's Tina. If for twenty eight years, practically day and night, you are referred to by a certain name, the subconscious mind eventually accepts it. I have memories of Anna Mae and the life Anna Mae lived, but I touch no part of that life at the moment. After I got my divorce and I stepped into my own, there was no ghost of the past. Everything surrounding me is always Tina. I have nothing in my house from the past. I have old photographs of the family, but I only look at them because that's as close as getting to your ancestors as you can. The country girl is just a memory. Somehow, all that time, I had all this happening in my head. It was always fantasy and Hollywood and hair and my mother's makeup. So when I did finally become that, working as much as I work, it's natural to wake up in the morning Tina.

WHAT IT'S LIKE GOING THROUGH LIFE WITH A NAME SOMEONE YOU NO LONGER LIKE GAVE YOU

When Ike first gave me the name I didn't like it, not until I came to Europe and heard it pronounced correctly; I thought it was a very pretty name, for stage. Then when I was divorced, I took nothing but my name, because I felt I had earned it. That name Tina opened doors. I did make a name for myself with that name. That name went on my driver's license, my passport. That name's my heritage, my trademark.

A TRUTH FURTHEST FROM THE TRUTH

"Women end up marrying their fathers." Ike was nothing like my father—physically. My father was a beautiful man. I was not close to my him and I felt he didn't like me, but I remember everything about him. He was very proud and very neat, even when he was working in the cotton fields. He wore the proper hightop shoes and his overalls were always washed and

ironed. He did have one hat that had sweat marks; but that was all that was unfresh about him. Psychically, Ike and my farther were more similar. My father fought my mother and Ike fought with his women. Strangely enough, it was a karma for me to get trapped in that kind of existence. But I knew I had to break that. Since my divorce I have not had a man strike me or even come near it. Ike should not have been my boyfriend or my husband.

WHAT I THOUGHT WHEN I FIRST SAW IKE

I thought that he was terribly ugly, and he was. After we got together I changed him a bit. He had a bad dental set and a thin mustache and he was wearing a process. But he had a great structure to his face, and I felt, if only if he could show that. In the end he did and he was quite attractive. He had a flat kind of body, similar to how David Bowie looks in his suits. He always chose good clothing for himself, but was very bad with things for his face and hair.

A TRUTH THAT'S TRUE

"I taught Mick Jagger to dance." That's actually true, because Mick wasn't dancing when I toured with him in 1966. I didn't know who he was and I thought he had a very strange face. It was like a baby face, a really white, white-face boy with big lips who was always standing in the wings behind the speaker, looking at me. When I'm on stage, I don't look that much, but when I see something strange, I remember it. Finally I said to Ike, "Who is that with the really strange face?" Then Ike brought Mick into the room and Mick said, "I like to watch you girls dance." So we—the Ikettes, Mick and I—started to play around with dancing, doing the pony and those steps. After that he started to move around on stage. The whole trip was a lot of him in our dressing room. We locked into each other immediately. I definitely feel that Mick and I knew each other in another lifetime.

MEN I WOULDN'T MIND LOOKING LIKE

William Hurt; Harrison Ford, a bit. I don't like them too pretty or cute. Sean Connery is visually the type of man I'd want to take on.

WHAT I WOULD HAVE BEEN IF I WERE WHITE
A child star

47

Jonathan Richman &

HOW THE MODERN LOVERS GOT ITS NAME
Jonathan Richman:
We wanted a name for a rock 'n' roll band that
wouldn't be just another name, but would describe the
group. We chose the Modern Lovers because we sing
modern love songs.

The Modern Lovers

WHAT IS OLD LOVE

The whole Casanova thing. Don Juan trying to get as many girls as he can. He's proud of fucking girls. He likes the power and the whole ego thing of sex. I think that form of love really isn't love. People don't distinguish between love and the ego thing of sex.
Here you have Don Juan, the young lover, and let's say his idea of a beautiful woman walked by. He says, "I must have you." In other words, "I love you." That's my idea of horseshit.

WHAT THE GIRL SAYS

"Don't you care about what I want?"
"What do you mean you love me?"
"You mean you want to do what you want to me."

WHAT DON JUAN SAYS

"I could show you new things."

AND SHE SAYS

"Yeah, but suppose I'm not ready for it?" If Don Juan was really together and liked himself, he would know when a girl wants and needs him; he won't have to tell her. He won't have to convince her. There she is. All this convincing is forcing the issue.

WHAT I MEAN BY MODERN LOVE

The time when you don't have to force the issue.
When you don't have to prove anything to yourself.
When you think you're all right.
When you don't need sex to feel all right.

MY KIND OF WOMAN

Well, I like all girls, but as far as my kind of woman goes, if there is any, it is a woman who has a fire inside she's in touch with and doesn't waste any time expressing it.

MY IDEA OF A DREAM DATE

A date where you spend the whole time dreaming. It's at night, under the stars. I could be right here.
Or near Chinatown in New York, overlooking the East River. A dream date would be trying to get closer to the dream. The girl and you both see the sky, which is a combination of that cobalt blue and that warmth and that cold that scares you and you want to fly

into it. This is what the guy thinks. And this is what the girl thinks. They are both thinking the same thing.

WHAT I'M THINKING (WHEN I WRITE A SONG)

A combination of what I think the girl's thinking and what I see guys thinking. Suppose I see a lot of guys feeling they're inferior because they don't fuck. That makes me write a song that says you're not inferior because you don't fuck. In fact, that would be the title of the song.

WHAT OUR AUDIENCE THINKS

Some of them are too shocked. Some of them are sure we're putting them on. Some of them can't hear the lyrics because we don't have a good P.A. system and don't worry about it. Some of them are too scared and don't know what's happening and can't even get that specific. But I want to do everything I can to let everyone know I'm serious.

WHY I CRY WHEN I SING

I'm so moved by my own singing. I'm almost crying now.

HOW I BECAME A MODERN LOVER

I went into this when I was sixteen and one of the reasons I started was that I knew I had no standard voice. I just wanted top show in a way that anyone could do it. Anyone. It didn't matter how pretty your voice was. All you had to have was feeling. People said it took courage to do what I did when I was performing alone and only knew two chords on the guitar, but it was just something I wanted to do so badly, no one could have stopped me.

HOW MODERN LOVERS DRESS

I like to dress on stage as close to what I wear on the street as possible. You don't have to dress up to be a Modern Lover. You don't have to do anything but express what you feel.

WHAT I DID BEFORE I WAS A MODERN LOVER

I was frustrated. I had no friends. I had big dreams. And even for a while during the early Lovers stages I had these problems.

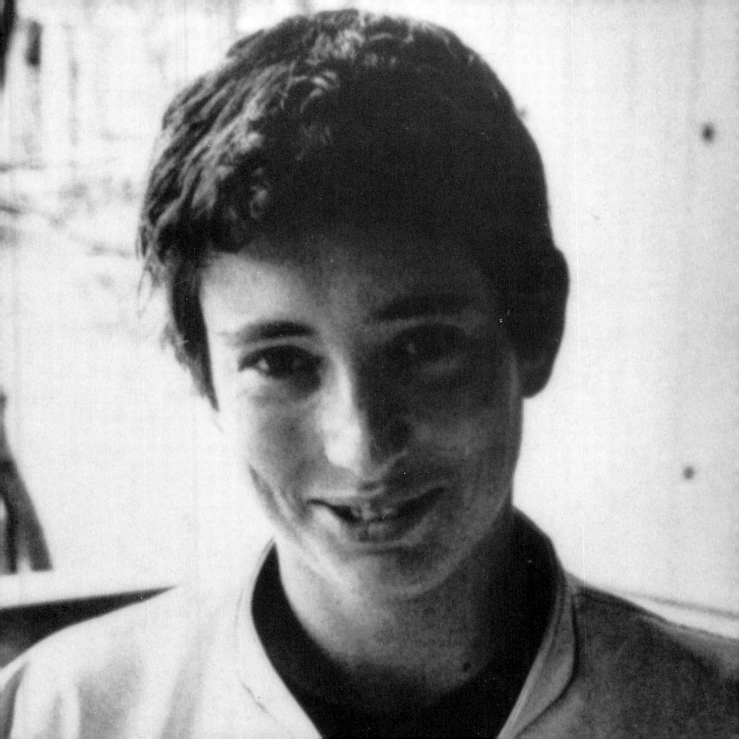

MUSIC I LISTENED TO THEN
Gospel music, the Velvet Underground, which I consider
gospel, Bulgarian music, any kind of
Slavic music, Staple Singers, Sam Cooke, Van Morrison,
Desmond Dekkar, '50s rock 'n'roll, twangy surf music

OTHER CULTURE HEROES
Lou Reed
Zalman Yanofsky—because of his stage presence
Babe Ruth—because he was magical, like the film of him
hitting his sixtieth home run on September 30, 1927
The movie *Patton*
The Boston Tea Party
Walter Johnson—"He would break a thousand hearts but
gave his own to only one."

WHY THE MODERN LOVERS DO WHAT WE DO
To be contrary. I want to dress in bright colors because it
makes me feel that pretty magic. I don't want
people to think we're prudes or some new round-head
religious sect. I like wearing a T-shirt on stage because
you can see my arms, and my arms tell you a lot
about the kind of work I do. I wear my hair short so you
can see my face. I wear sneakers. I'm just as tall as I appear.
Sneakers don't even have heels. Actually, it
helps my stage act to wear something I know someone else
hates. It makes me feel stronger. It makes me
feel persecuted. So I feel I have this power inside me and I
know, overcoming all obstacles, the Modern Lovers
are going to triumph.

THINGS THAT PREPARE ME TO GO ON STAGE
The Sufi Message of Hazrat Inayat Khan
The Aquarian Gospel of Jesus the Christ by Ha Levi
The Quality of Courage by Mickey Mantle
News clippings from the *National Enquirer* about courage,
like people who have cancer but are fighting it

WHAT I LOOK FOR IN A MANAGER
Someone who is moral and magical
Someone who would guide me spiritually
Someone who has that fire inside and
isn't afraid to let it out
Someone to tell us we're not playing enough orphanages

WHAT THE MODERN LOVERS HAVE TO LEARN
Spanish

THE FIRST TIME I SAW JONATHAN
David Robsinon:
In 1970, on the Cambridge Common, every Sunday there
was a free concert there. I think it was 1970.
Jonathan will know the date precisely. He'll know the date
of every event that ever happened. He didn't have a band
then. It was just him and he used to wear a
white plastic Harley-Davidson motorcycle jacket. That was
his trademark. People would say, "Did you see
that crazy guy with the white plastic jacket?" They'd say,
"We have young Johnny Richman coming up,"
and everybody would laugh and boo, but mostly ignore
him. He was funny and terrible, but he was aggressive and
wild compared to what else was going on. Some weeks
someone like the Grateful Dead or the Allman Brothers
would be there and in the middle of that
atmosphere, Jonathan would come out. Then one day he
walked into the record store where I worked. He was
starting a band and was putting a little card
up on the bulletin board in the store and he agreed right
then that I would be the drummer.

JONATHAN 'S IDEA ABOUT GIRLS
David:
I respected Jonathan on one hand, because it was noble, but
at the same time it was absurd and unrealistic. And in
his case, unhealthy.

WHAT WAS IT WITH JONATHAN AND GIRLS
Ernie Brooks:
Jonathan was one of those kids who was totally in his own
world. He did not know
how to talk to girls. He put them up on a pedestal. He'd
visit girls at night up on the astral plane.
Some of the girls he intercepts up there he may have
known from other lives. He'd call me up at six in the
morning and wake me up. "Ernie, I entered her dream last
night. I know I entered her dream. I don't know
if I should have done that." I'd say, "No Jonathan, that's
wrong. Don't do that."

WHAT HAPPENED WHEN THE BAND WENT TO BERMUDA

We had a friend at Harvard whose cousin managed this
hotel. We alternated with the Fiery Limbo
Dancers—they do the limbo with flaming sticks and roll
around on broken glass without getting hurt—and
the Esso Steel Band, and we drove all the tourists out of the
room each time we played. It was also an omen
of things to come. We all slept in one room and Jonathan
used to snore, so we put dirty socks in his mouth
to shut him up.

WHAT HAPPENED WITH MISS CHRISTINE

She was one of the G.T.O.s, Frank Zappa's group of Girls
Together Outrageously—John Cale's wife Cindy was also
in it. She flew out from L.A.—that was
November or December of '72—and came to visit us in this
great old house outside Boston that I had gone to great
lengths to rent from this ambassador who made
us promise that we'd be very moral, clean, and have no
drugs. Then Miss Christine brought a whole pharmacy of
drugs with her and apparently she shot up and
O.D.ed the first night she was there. Within a week we had
to move out of that house.

WHAT WAS WITH THE MODERN LOVERS AND MANAGERS
Jerry Harrison:

We asked them about their politics and what books they
read, but as much as anything it was what their morality
was. We thought of ourselves as a cause
and we didn't want to be ruined by something that would
ruin what we were trying to accomplish. Which
meant all the managers that didn't have much success
seemed in some ways more attractive. Whereas
someone like David Geffen seemed sullied by his success.
So we went around in circles through the summer
of '72 and into '73. Eventually we went with these
managers until they had us play for
Lee Michaels and Tower of Power in San Bernardino,
where when we went into "When you get out
of the hospital, will you let me back into your life?" the
audiences started throwing things at us and the managers
got very scared and backed out.

Ernie:

First we rejected the good managers and by the time we
realized we needed one of those good managers we proved
ourselves so difficult that most of those good managers
wouldn't have touched us.

WHAT HAPPENED IN CALIFORNIA
Ernie:

It was the summer of '73. We signed with Warner Bros.—
they had a reputation for taking on new, unusual acts and
also rock 'n' roll acts—and
drove out to California to record with John Cale, who was
a staff producer. We were all big friends of
the Velvet Underground and John Cale was a legend to us.
In Las Vegas it was 117-degrees and all our records
warped and all the guitar necks got bent by the heat.
We got to California and we moved into Emmylou Harris's
house in Van Nuys. It was almost as soon as we got there
that things started to fall apart. We recorded a
couple of tracks with Cale. He kept trying to get Jonathan
to play violently. He'd say, "Jonathan, you got to attack the
guitar. You got to sound mean." Jonathan was
starting to go into this state of mind where he'd go, "No, I
don't want to be mean, I want to be nice." He was starting
to grow up a little bit and was coming out of his adolescent
angst. As far as we were concerned, this was
causing problems with his music. The three of us would

say, "Look Jonathan, how we got this far was on this kind of a sound. We can't start changing it now." We were trying to do the old songs—that's the sound Cale had heard and wanted to produce—and Jonathan was trying to sweeten them up and make them more acoustic. It's around that time he wrote "Government Center," "The Bank Teller," and "A Plea for Tenderness." So we started having fights in the studio with Cale and decided this wasn't working. Then Kim Fowley came along with this bubbly, dumb enthusiasm. He'd yell "Make it teenage!" from the control room. It helped in that there was no argument. Everything we did he said was great. So we recorded a bunch of stuff with him that we ended up not being so satisfied with, but then it got to the point where David couldn't stand to be in the same room as Jonathan. Problem was that Warner Bros. would call up everyday trying to figure out if we found a manager yet, what was going on with the recording. At one point Jonathan said we were going to finish the record, but when we went on tour we wouldn't play any of the songs that were going to be on the album. Of course one of the things a record company who is going to put money into an album wants is to promote the album. This was also around the time Jonathan decided he didn't like electricity. He thought electricity was evil because it consumed natural resources to create it and only acoustic instruments could be used. And if acoustic instruments were used, they didn't make much noise, then you couldn't use a P.A., then you really couldn't use drums.

David:
After we went out to L.A. and the whole record thing fell apart, I just felt I had enough. Jonathan was obsessed with the acoustic and playing street corners, rest homes, and orphanages and I was supposed to bang a rolled up newspaper against my fist as percussion.

Jerry:
After David said he had it—the fall of '73—we drove back to Boston. We kind of reformed the band with Bob Turner playing drums and we played our last job in the spring of '74. Everyone loved it; then Jonathan said, "You're too loud" and "People like 'Roadrunner' too much" and wouldn't play it. That's when the band ended finally.

Ernie:
In retrospect, I think Jonathan was right. Maybe we were just too uptight. We were into being in this cool rock 'n' roll band and going "buzz, buzz" in the background of this cute little insect song—"Hey There, Little Insect." It didn't fit the image we had of ourselves. Maybe we should have followed Jonathan into his vision a little more.

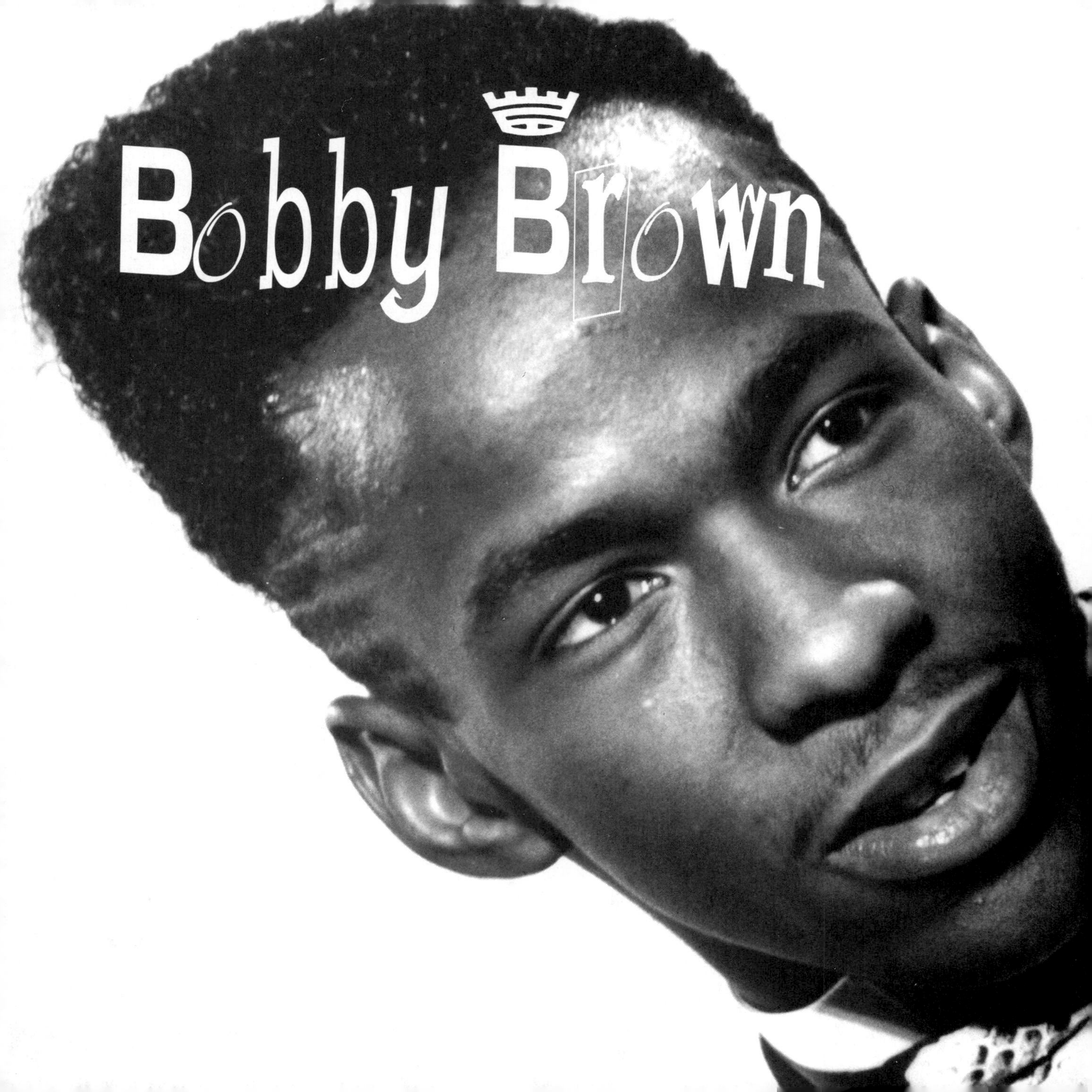
Bobby Brown

WHAT I DO WHEN I MEET SOMEONE FOR THE FIRST TIME
Look at their shoes. If the shoes are neat, it says this person takes care of himself. I'm one person who can't go out of the house with a pair of dirty shoes. Once they get a spot on them, I'm ready to throw them out.

WHAT I LOOK FOR IN A PAIR OF SHOES
Something that'll make my feet look small, usually something with a round toe. I prefer suede shoes with small leather heels and thick rubber soles, like the Bally hightops most rappers wear. I got them in all different colors because my outfit's not complete unless the shoes match.

SOMEONE'S SHOES I'D LIKE TO BE IN FOR A MOMENT
Eddie Murphy's, just to see what it's like to be the top box office draw in the world.

SOMEONE'S PANTS I'D LIKE TO GET INTO
Janet Jackson's

SOMEONE'S PANTS I'M IN NOW
Richard Tyler's; he's out of Los Angeles. My pants most definitely have to be baggy, but tight at the bottom—about six inches above the ankles—and end just above the shoes

WHAT I WEAR UNDER MY PANTS
Usually a regular pair of Hanes boxer shorts, whether striped, checkered, or with hearts

SOMETHING NO CLOSET SHOULD BE WITHOUT
A rack that turns around, like at the cleaners

MY FIRST FASHION INFLUENCES
Teddy Pendergrass—he was *the* ladies' man back then—and Charlie Johnson, a local hustler from out of Boston

MY BEST-DRESSED LIST
Eddie Murphy
New Edition
Guy
Big Daddy Kane

SOMETHING I WEAR WHEN I WANT TO LOOK SEXY
A red silk robe with black satin trim and nothing underneath

SOMETHING I WEAR WHEN I HAVE NOTHING TO SAY
A hip-hop costume—a hat on backwards, glasses, and a sweatsuit.

SOMETHING I WOULDN'T BE CAUGHT DEAD IN
A sombrero

57

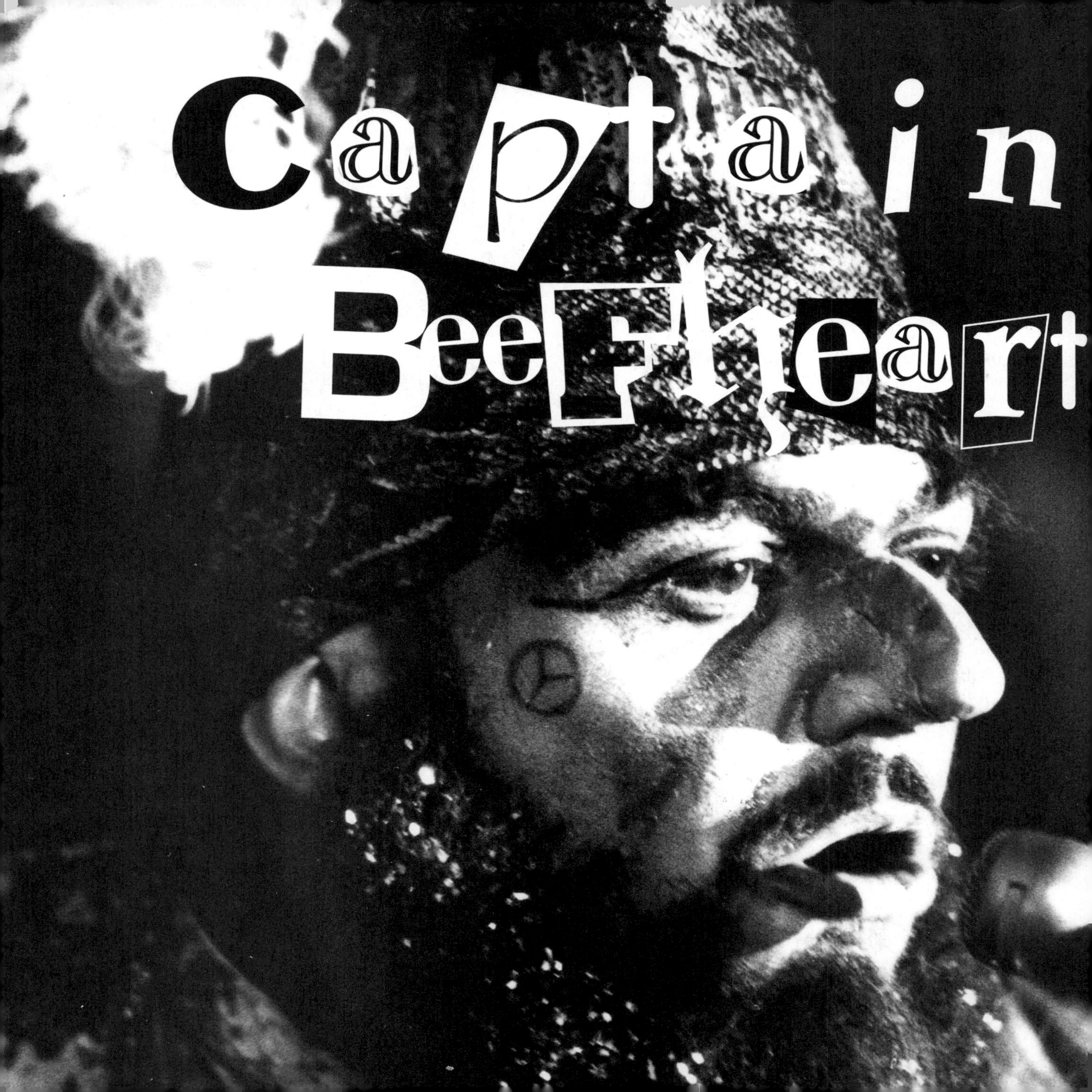
Captain
Beefheart

HOW I GOT MY NAME
There was a black gentleman selling tomatoes and his name was The Captain. He would say, "My tomatoes are as big as beefhearts." Captain Beefheart is a shingle that I assure you has given me shingles at times because of the fact that I'm vegetarian.

SOMETHING I HATE
Music. I always have. It was an allergy or an irritation that I had to soothe. I'm very serious about painting, however.

SOME NOTABLE EXCEPTIONS
Howlin' Wolf, around 1954

John Coltrane, when McCoy Tyner was in his band, around the time John F. Kennedy was assassinated

The Andrews Sisters, when they sang "Money Is the Root of All Evil"

Son House, one of the most underrated people in music. All he had was a cigar box and guitar. And he was just excellent at clearing his throat.

MY LEAST FAVORITE ERA IN HISTORY
Disco

A PHOTOGRAPH I'D LIKE TO HAVE BEEN IN
I don't know if I wish I were in one, but I sure like Diane Arbus. Some of her things were so good it was just ridiculous. I don't think she thought those people she was shooting were freaks. I don't think there is such a thing as freaks. I'm surprised, there was never a punk band called the Diane Arbus Band.

customized with lace or tulle. But I wish I was flat-chested and didn't have to wear a bra. It's one extra piece of clothing to worry about.

WHAT TURNS ME ON

Skin, lips, and Latin men. I'm also attracted to bums. Once, when I went to Paris, I hung out with Algerians and Vietnamese guys who didn't have jobs, who just drove around on motorcycles and terrorized people. I've always been attracted to people like that, who are rebels, an irresponsible challenge to the norm. I try to rehabilitate them. I'm just trying to be the mother I never had.

WHAT TURNS ME OFF

I wouldn't want to sleep with a guy who was a virgin. I'd have to teach him stuff and I don't have the patience. I'd rather deal with experience. When I say virgin, like in my song, I'm not thinking about sexual virgin. I mean newness. Even after I made love for the first time, I still felt I was a virgin. I didn't lose my virginity until I knew what I was doing.

THE PROBLEM WITH BOYFRIENDS

I wish I was a million different people so I could stay with each boyfriend while moving onto the next. I learn more, want more, and suddenly, that person isn't enough. The problem is, after you start to love someone, you hurt them. I get interested in somebody else and I latch onto that interest to get me through the other one. It's painful, but then I have this new guy to look forward to.

Al Green

SONGS THAT INFLUENCED ME MOST
"You Send Me," Sam Cooke
"My Girl," the Temptations

THREE THINGS I RECENTLY BOUGHT AT BLOOMINGDALE'S
Silk slacks
A sweater the color of creativity (brush red)
A pair of cotton socks

WORDS THAT BEST DESCRIBE ME
Rain bath

MY DREAM CAR
One of those wreck- 'em-up '75 Corvettes with dark glasses

A MAGAZINE I NEVER MISS
Elle

SOMETHING I USED TO DO BUT DON'T ANY LONGER
Go down into my basement and lock myself in my room.
Now I go and sit out by the pool.

THE NEAREST FARAWAY PLACE
My Corvette

WHERE MY SONGS COME FROM
A special place I've never told anyone about
that has no lock on the door and I've only been to once

MY HOROSCOPE
"Discretion shall preserve thee and understanding shall keep thee."

DaVid Byrne

RECORDS THAT MATTERED

Cold Sweat, James Brown
The Who Sell Out, the Who
Trout Mask Replica, Captain Beefheart

THREE FAVORITE B-SIDES

"Double-Dutch Bus"
"How Are We Going to Make That Black Nation Rise"
"Nancy Reagan"—a reggae song about Nancy Reagan's
dresses

POP STARS I WANTED TO LOOK LIKE

The Grateful Dead
Dexter Gordon—He has an amazing sense of cool that
comes across during live performances.

THE FIRST POP STAR I WANTED TO FUCK

Mia Farrow—She wasn't a pop star but she was once
married to Frank Sinatra.

MOVIES I'VE SEEN IN ONE DAY

The Abyss
Star Trek
Indiana Jones and the Temple of Doom
Commando

FAVORITE BOOK OF POETRY

Bean Spasms, by Ted Berrigan and Ron Padget

THE WOMAN I'D MOST LIKE TO BE LIKE

Tallulah Bankhead

MOST VALUED POSSESSIONS

An automatic pencil that I got in Berlin and
I think I've since lost

HOW I'D KNOW A GIRL WAS RIGHT FOR ME

I'd think, Could I ride on a Greyhound bus with
this person?

SOMEONE I WOULDN'T MIND BEING FOR A MOMENT

Ryszard Kapuscinski. He wrote *The Emperor and the Sha of
Shas* and witnessed twenty-seven political
revolutions. To have seen some of the stuff he has seen
and lived to tell about it is pretty amazing. The guy must
have a charmed life.

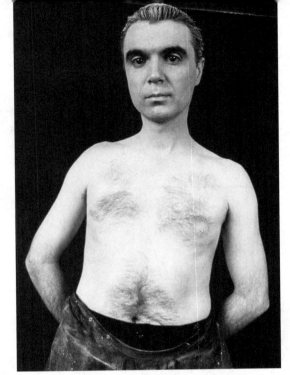

AN HISTORICAL EVENT I WISH I WITNESSED

I don't think of history as a board game where you can go
from this event to that event—things get nudged one way
or another—but I'd like to have witnessed the burning
bush or Joshua blowing his horn and the walls of
Jerico tumbling down. When you think of it, it must have
been like an Indiana Jones movie.

AN HISTORICAL EVENT I'D LIKE TO FORGET

Man landing on the moon. I watched the rebroadcast
twenty years later and the whole first hour and a half was
one shot of mission control. The camera never moved, you
just heard the astronauts' voices over their radio. Then,
finally, the big moment comes when they flick on
the camera and you see a picture of the leg of the spaceship
for a couple of hours. It was like an Andy Warhol movie.

A pair of sandals that old men wear in Paris that I don't
think I could find anywhere else—but I think it would be
pretty dumb to grow attached to a pair of sandals.

The hat my parents had made for me by a
hatter in Baltimore

WHERE I HANG MY HAT
Not in the overhead bin of an airplane

MY SECRET FOR SUCCESS
My point of view might sound naive, but if you're honest and sincere in what you're doing, then there's a good chance that there are people out there who feel the same way, and even with a minimum of skill and technique, if you're honest and sincere, these people will find out about you through some mysterious process.

HOW LONG YOU SHOULD WAIT
The Talking Heads were very lucky. I expected it to take about five years for people to find out about us and it took around two. I've spoken to other people who took much longer, like twenty years, before their audience increased to beyond fifty people. There's a good way and a bad way of looking at that. Obviously you shouldn't persist at something if no one's interested. But part of the object of doing something is to get your ideas across to other people, so you got to make some effort.

WHAT I WAS TRAINED TO DO
My father worked for Westinghouse as an electrical engineer, so I leaned toward that sort of thing, but art seemed to be more fun, so I went with the art, though I had a non-art way of looking at things. I didn't know how things would end up. Being in a band was the most fun and when we started to attract attention, I automatically made a decision.

A JOB I HAD BEFORE JOINING A BAND
A hash slinger—in the Yankee Clipper Diner in Rhode Island, but I didn't survive too many breakfast shifts; at 7:30 fifty people would yell out their orders as they walked in the door. They didn't even wait until they sat down.

CONTROLLING MY SINGING VOICE
My singing voice is not my natural voice. It seems to jump up there when I sing because I get excited. I think, with more practice, I'll be able to sing in my natural voice and then I might be able to convey more emotions, rather than everything being a squeal, which gives the song the wrong impression. Sometimes I want to sing words that are very heartfelt, but they come out sounding like I'm being strangled.

HOW FAMOUS PEOPLE DRESS
I used to think all famous people dressed pretty strange. The most famous bands on TV wore suits. The Rolling Stones wore bell-bottoms and weird shirts with scarves, and I couldn't imagine myself wearing those clothes. Soul bands had suits and gloves that glowed in the dark. I really couldn't imagine myself wearing that either. The only thing I could imagine doing was dressing extremely modular. Either that or looking like a cowboy.

WHAT I'D WEAR IF I WERE BEING PHOTOGRAPHED FOR POSTERITY

Just a shirt and a pair of pants, but I'd take extra care that they photographed me well. Maybe I'd have a big dinner in front of me. Maybe I'd be watching TV and have a magazine lying around, to write things down on. Either that, or I'd like a group portrait with about fifty friends around, like "These Are My Friends."

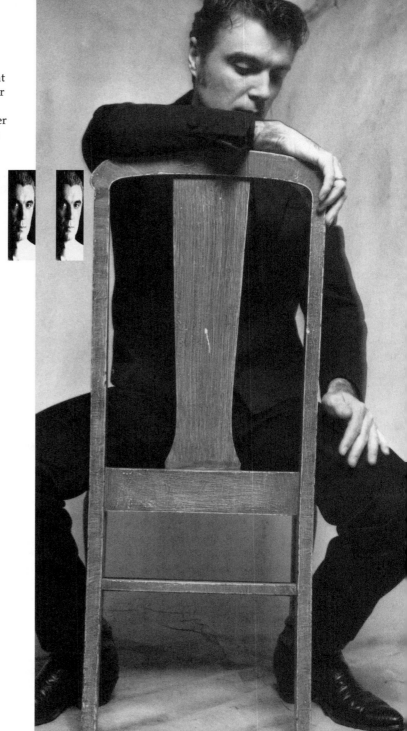

Malcolm McLaren

A ROOM I'D LIKE TO ROOM IN

John Keats' room, with the flowers painted on the ceiling, in the Piaza di Spagna in Rome, just before he died. He always imagined himself dying with all those flowers falling on top of him. It was the ultimate erotic suicide.

THREE FLOWERS I'D LIKE TO BE CRUSHED TO DEATH BY

Lilies
Roses
Forget-me-nots

MY FAVORITE EPITAPH

"Here lies a man whose name was written in water."

ROCK STARS I WISH I INVENTED

Eddie Cochran and Gene Vincent. I'm such an oddball, though, that I would never have met anybody as talented as they were. I only meet people who can't do anything but want to do something, although, at the end of the day, I've represented the gods in some shape or form with the Sex Pistols.

TWO RECORDS THAT INFLUENCED ME MOST

Johann Strauss' overture to *Die Fledemaus*. I thought a lot about it when I made *Fans* and *Waltz Darling*

Gene Vincent singing "Somewhere Over the Rainbow." There was something so fantastically incongruous about him doing it and at the same time so romantically tragic. I first heard it fifteen years ago when I opened a teddy boy shop on King's Road; the last time I played it was when I moved to Hollywood and met Lauren Hutton and suddenly decided to buy some records for the apartment. I always went for the soppy songs.

THE FIRST RECORD I BOUGHT

"Heart and Soul," by Jan and Dean

TWO CHILDREN I WISH I HAD

Madonna and Melanie Griffith

A TRUTH THAT IS NOT TRUE

Musicians are at the cutting edge of our culture. They are followers; music's not a leader's medium; it's painters who are always in advance of the mood of the times. Musicians tend to be behind and struggling to catch up because they're inside waiting to hear and read about that information.

HOW I SEE MUSIC

Being an artist in a medium I am not prepared in, I make music a little like a painter would make music or a film director would. I go out and look at music, rather than play it. If a musician walks down a street and sees a building he will never see that building; he will only hear the sound around it. I will be constantly concerned about the facade. That is a very different way of conceptualizing things because we are always aware of the facade in the world and its constant change and moods.

MY FAVORITE NAME FOR A BAND

The last word in Edie Brickell and the New Bohemians

SOMEONE I'D LOVE TO DESIGN CLOTHES FOR

Sylvester Stallone. I don't know how I'd dress him, but I would definitely give him a pipe.

WHERE I LIVE

In my dreams; I have always refused to live in reality. Right now I'm being truly cursed for it. I've been cursed for it earlier on, but I'm paying for it like hell right now. It's a rough road to keep going down and for one reason or another, I don't seem to be able to change.

DREAMS I'D LIKE TO BE IN

The most political and powerful's. I'd feel very sexy being in their dreams because I'd either by the annoying germ or hopefully the most moving. If I'm ever to be considered a poet in my lifetime, it's only going to be in some politician's dream or nightmare.

UP UNTIL NOW

I feel my whole life has been that of a kept woman.

HOW I'D LIKE TO BE

I used to be proud of being the ultimate brat but now I want to be a bit more useful. You can't fall in love unless you feel useful. I want to be in love, but the more you try, the more you'll never find it.

THE NEAREST FARAWAY PLACE

Cuba. It lies somewhere in my body. I don't have any genuine English blood; I'm half Spanish-Portuguese-Jewish and half Scottish, although the Scottish part comes from Cuba. My grandfather was born in Havana, and my ancestors lived in Havana. The McLaren clan emigrated there to escape the wrath of the English when they invaded Scotland in 1810, and my grandfather emigrated back to England at the turn of the century. I've always been attracted to things Latin and only found out why recently when I met my father for the first time since birth.

SOMETHING I WAS AFRAID TO REVEAL ABOUT MYSELF IN THE PAST

I never wanted to reveal the existence of my past. Now I'm very concerned to fill up that hole and create my past in order to become, before it's too late, a little real. That's why I made a conscious effort to find my father. Lauren Hutton persuaded me to make the effort. I exposed the idea across the entire British Isles through all the daily and weekly press. That's how I discovered that he was alive, which I didn't know, and that he was living in England; his fifth wife saw the notice and informed the newspaper that I should contact him through her. I met my father on a marsh, in an old dilapidated cottage on the site where *Great Expectations* was literally written. When I arrived, he was already there waiting in the shadows for ten minutes while I stood alone wondering what the hell was going on. He looked like something out of the movies; he didn't look anything like me. He was extraordinarily suave, weary, suspicious, and a little guilty. He knew everything about me and I didn't know anything about him. He didn't want to talk about himself, but I did find out that I had another brother and sister who are professors up at Cambridge University who I never knew existed. I'm going up to see them next. My brother is a man who talks to trees. My father also showed me photographs of all my ancestors from Havana.

I was silent most of the time; I just looked at him, at his deeply creviced face, his tiny moustache and golden yellow wavy hair and a very debonair emerald green silk shirt and white trousers. I saw things in him that I didn't like in myself: extreme votility; self-obsessed; very unwilling to show affection easily; a person who is as much a dreamer as I have been and has been fairly caddish about life. I suddenly felt it wasn't healthy for me to be like that, although let's face it all the characters we adore in life's dramas are the most irresponsible spoiled brats: Don Giovanni, Casanova, Don Juan, Mick Jagger, rock 'n' roll.

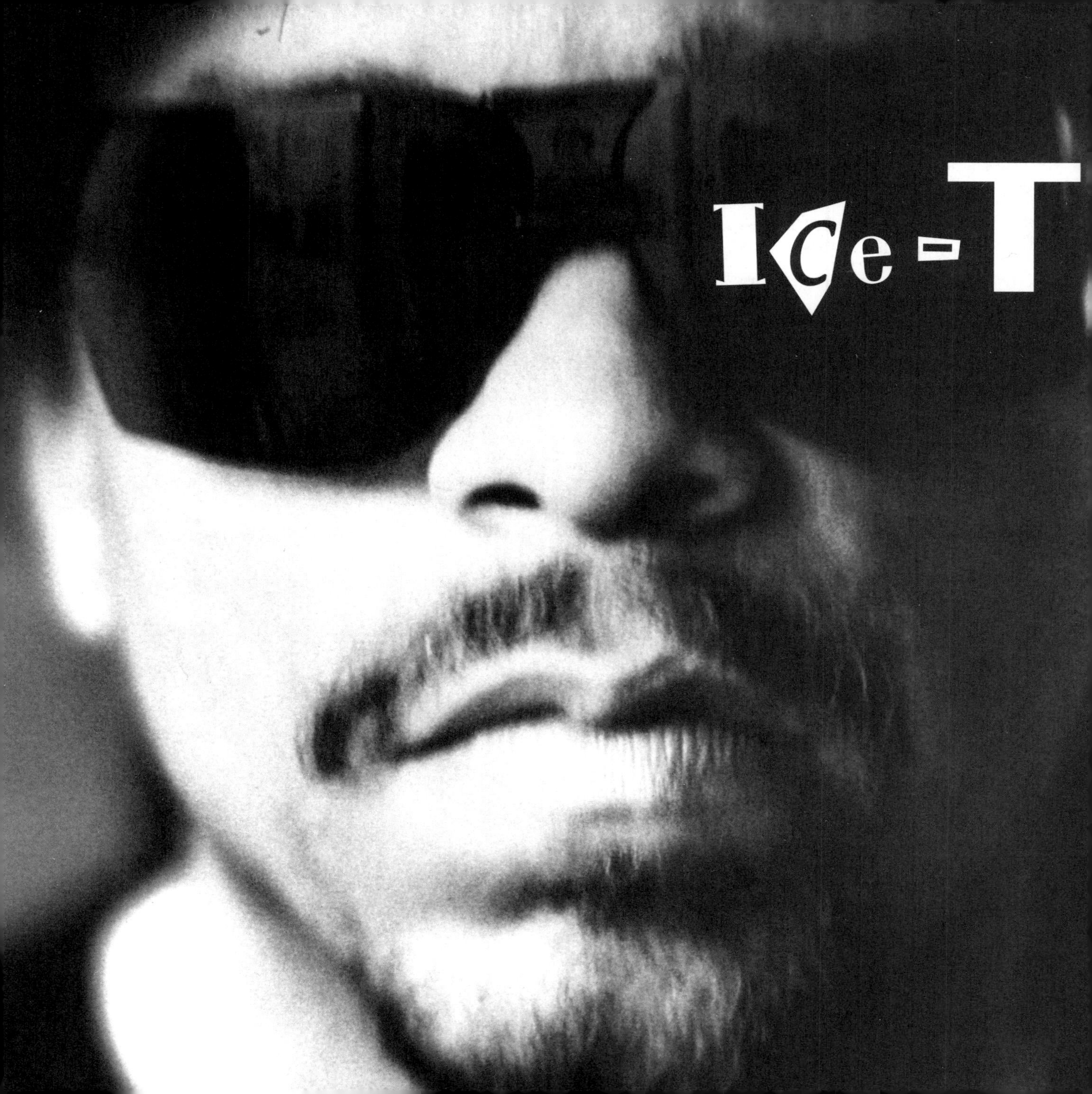
Ice-T

THE WHITE PERSON I IDENTIIFIED WITH MOST
Dennis the Menace

TV SHOWS I WATCHED AS A KID
"Ozzie and Harriet"
"Leave It to Beaver"
"My Three Sons"

WHY I STOPPED WATCHING
After awhile you can't watch these shows because you don't have as much furniture as them; it's another world. And I don't know anybody living like the Cosbys, who's got a father who's a doctor and a mother who's a lawyer and nobody get whippings. Even the Flintstones are white. The only cool cartoons, the only cartoons with soul, were Bugs Bunny and Daffy Duck. They were definitely black. They have a different attitude than the Cleavers. I was always violence oriented. I believe when nothing on TV is about you, you can always resort to violence because violence is what you know.

MOVIES I SNUCK INTO AS A KID
Karate and horror films. Once me and my crew snuck into a triple feature with *Old Yeller* on the bill and we all puked. Basically we'd go into a movie to talk to girls and steal purses. I didn't sit in the movies to absorb film. I still have some of the worst taste in America as far as films go.

LAST TWO VIDEOS I RENTED
Bloodbath Stewardesses and
Texas Chainsaw School Girls

MY FAVORITE ROLE MODEL
Cher—She can do Karen Silkwood and come off very conservative, then be butt naked on a battleship. The key is to do both well.

BANDS I WAS INTO
Parliament. I was hypnotized by the Mothership. Black Sabbath. I liked that evil-sounding stuff. Judas Priest. I was into anything that was supposed to be bad.

FAVORITE POP FASHION IDOL
James Brown, the Godfather. He was the first with a gangsta style.

HOW I GOT MY START
Originally I was a drag artist, a talker. I'd come into your jewelry store and I'd have some jewelry and say, "I'm interested in a 3.2 karat diamond; my parents are out here in the area buying condominiums and I'm a pre-law student and this is like their twentieth anniversary and my dad already has one of those Rolexes. Can I see that Piaget number, the one that's parve?" And they'd hand me like thousands of dollars of watches and I'd just run out of the store.

MY BEST MOVE
We had this credit card printer—this was before they had holograms—and we'd take old credit cards and press them with new numbers that we'd pull off those credit card commercials on TV. I don't think those numbers had a limit on them.

SOME PLACES I'VE GONE TO ON CREDIT CARDS
Jamaica
Miami
Korea
All the cities the L.A. Raiders have played

MY CURRENT RECORD
15 arrests,
0 convictions

A COUPLE OF PLACES I'D LIKE TO MAKE LOVE
On an iceberg
On a roller coaster

MY BEST PICKUP LINE
"Would you like to be on an album cover?"

THE BEST WAY TO LET A GIRL DOWN EASY
If you got a few girl friends, just put them together and the weak one will get out.

MY TWO MOST VALUED POSSESSIONS
A pit bull named Felony and an English bull dog named Chopper

MY FAVORITE PIECE OF JEWELRY
When I go out with Darlene. I don't have to dress; she's like jewelry.

FAVORITE HOUSEHOLD CHORE

Vacuuming. Usually Darlene goes after the dust and I go after the dog hairs.

SOMETHING I DON'T DO

Windows

SOME THINGS I KEEP NEAR MY BED

H&K 9mm with laser sight
.357 Magnum
AR-15
9mm

SOMETHING I KEEP ABOVE MY BED

A mirror that was inspired by a motel room Darlene and I used to stay in called the Snooty Fox

HOW I LEARNED ABOUT INTERIOR DECORATING

When I turned from gangster into player and started stealing. I had to get educated to what really was fly. If you're stealing, you steal a Sony, not a Gold Star.

HOW I PAID FOR MY EDUCATION

With other people's credit cards

A CLUB I BELONG TO

The Beverly Hills Gun Club

CARS IN MY GARAGE

A customized metallic blue '76 Porche Targa
with a 3.3 turbo engine,
steel slant nose, steel flairs, and convertible top

A two-tone candy '86 Mundial Ferrari with chrome wheels that's worth about $150,000 now that Enzo Ferrari died

A silver '31 steel body Ford hot rod with a Mustang suspension and engine—we take this out cruising on Sunset on a Friday night and it turns more heads than any other car

FAVORITE L.A. RESTAURANTS

Acapulco on Sunset near La Brea
Sizzlers—except there's too many cops sitting next to us
Red Lobster
Monty's—on top of a building in Westwood, where a lot of underworld figures and celebrities eat

SOME BOOKS ON MY BOOKSHELF

Iceberg Slim's. I read every one of his books.
Mama Black Widow
Death Wish
Black Gangster. I got my name from him.
Donald Goines Writes No More
Techniques of the Professional Pickpocket
How to Hide Anything
How to Make Disposable Silencers
Make 'Em Pay!
Various manuals on how to beat video games

THE BEST PIECE OF ADVICE MY FATHER GAVE ME

My father was slightly involved in the life. He worked a job, but he was probably selling dope on the side; he was the kind of guy who would be in the pool hall. He used to say, "Whatever you're going to do, you got to be professional about it. If you're going to be a crook, don't do it half the time, do it all the time. And if you're

77

going to be straight, be straight; don't try no slick shit." Now that I decided to make this transition to go straight, my mind ain't clicking like it used to.

MY FAVORITE PIECE OF ART
My aquarium—I'll bet if you went to any Mafia boss's house, he'd have flowers and butterflies around. The guns are there, but even the Godfather died fucking around with his grandson in the rosebushes. After all the violence, you have to chill.

FISH IN ICE-T'S TANK
(*According to John from Fish Art*)
Ice has puffers, angels—a blue face and an annularis—tangs, surgeon fish, and a moray eel that he's had since I've been taking care of the aquarium. Ice pays $125 a month and we provide everything from the fish to the coral to the tank itself. The fish are guaranteed for thirty days.

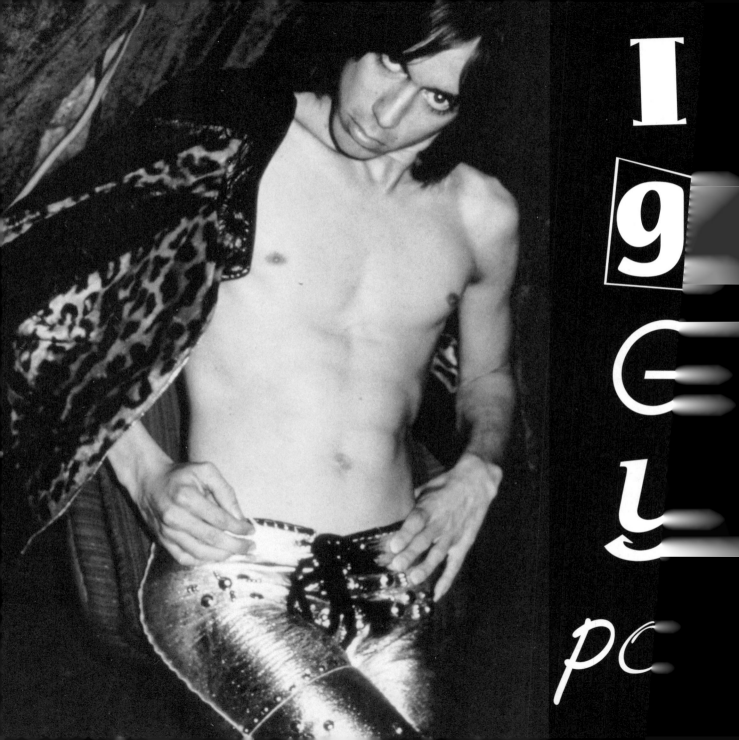

WHAT TO CALL ME

You can call me Iggy or you can call me Jimmy. My parents called me James Osterberg, Jr. Iggy was a nickname hung on me—that I didn't particularly like—when I was in high school and was in a band called the Iguanas. Iggy is short for Iguana. When I was eighteen I was in a band called the Prime Movers, an effete, Bohemian, intellectual blues band of twentyfive-and twentysix year-olds. About a year and a half after the Prime Movers I formed the Stooges and thought I had heard the last of that nickname. However, with the very first Stooges gig we played in 1968, which was second bill to Blood, Sweat and Tears, a local reviewer devoted most of his review to the Stooges, saying Blood, Sweat and Tears are a packaged act who have passed their prime, and the real story tonight came from a local band, the Stooges, fronted by vocalist Iggy Osterberg. The name's catchy and pretty soon people know me by it, so I stuck with it. Then I thought I'd tag a good last name onto it, because this sounded like show business, so I came up with Pop. When I begin a professional relationship, often I'm called Iggy, although the president of my record company calls me Jim. The credit card company calls me James. When my father's in a good mood he calls me Iggy, just to hassle me. Occasionally he calls me Jimbo and sometimes my wife does, too. My audience calls me Iggy, but groupies always call me Jim, because Iggy's not a mantic name. It's a dangerous name. It's the kind of name that, when shouted across a room, makes nice people wince. It's a dangerous game being called Iggy, no question about it. I'm really proud to be Iggy Pop, but if someone's more comfortable calling me Jim, that's fine, too.

MY MAJOR ROLE MODELS

The Renegades. When I was fourteen, they were the baddest group around. They were real thin, had bad skin, and wore shiny suits that were too tight. They were also mean and liked to fight. The drummer had psychotic episodes. I worshipped these guys. They performed at barn dances called sock hops, where on one bill you'd have Jerry Lee Lewis—when he walked on stage, his hair was so bright yellow, it sent out bolts of light around the barn. He just sneered at everybody;

I never saw anybody sneer at an audience before. Then he walked over to the piano, raised up his legs, kicked the keys once, and growled, "I'm not playing that shit," and walked off. There was a minute of chaos. Then he came back on and mimed the B-side of one of his records, which wasn't even a rock song, and split. I was in awe. Before the star performers went on there were two or three local greaser bands—real bands playing real music—and the Renegades were one of them. To me real rock 'n' roll was the local bands from the worst part of town. And the women I looked up to were local versions of the Shangri-Las and Ronnie Spector; they wore a big beehive hairdo, nylons, skirts with the slit in the back, bit pointy bars, and a big ring around their neck.

The Decibels—a greaser band led by Bob Seger. After I heard some of their stuff, I wanted to try it myself. I got a set of drums and started a two-man group called the Megaton 2, and entered the junior high talent show. The guitar player was a Duane Eddy freak and I was a Sandy Nelson freak; we played an instrumental version of Ray Charles's "What Did I Say, " and "Let There Be Drums," I got much more popular at school; girls who didn't talk to me started talking to me. Then, when I got to the tenth grade and got the Iguanas together and played fraternities, I started to realize you can get girls drunk and they'll do anything. That's also when criming started to come in. While the guys were all partying, it was tempting to go up to their rooms and steal their clothes.

Bob Dylan. I was about sixteen or seventeen and going out with an older woman who had friends who were considered beatniks. I had never seen anything like these people. They wore engineer boots, flannel shirts, and long hair. I was dreaming about being in a rock 'n' roll band and they were dreaming about being on a freight train. But this girl turned me on to the *Free Wheelin'* Bob Dylan album. I had never heard of a talking blues. And at the time, I had literary ambitions; I won twenty-five dollars for a poem I had written that a girl friend of mine had entered in a literary contest. I saw Dylan at a concert where he did the first half acoustic, all by himself, then took a fifteen-minute break. He reappeared wearing a grey Edwardian suit and a

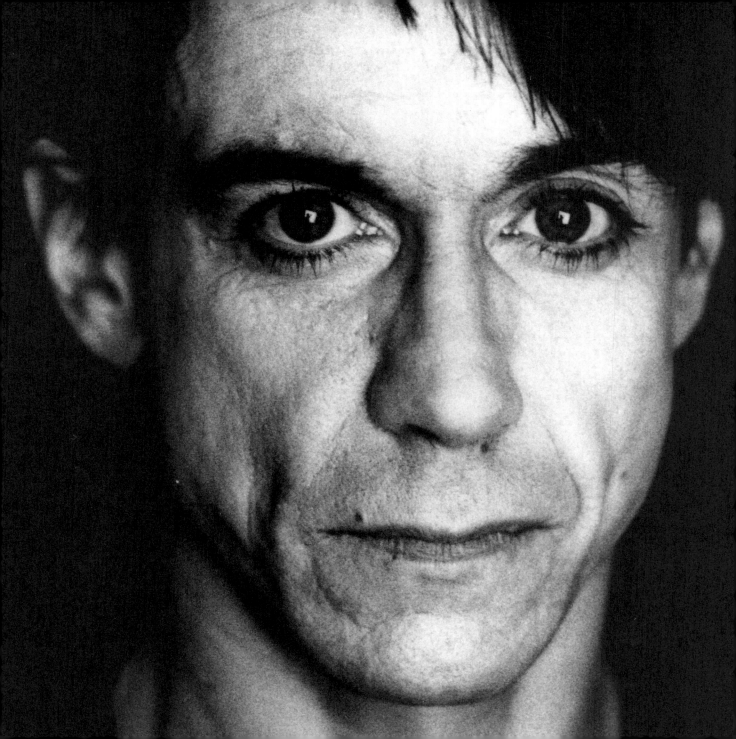

Stratocaster, his back to the audience, jumped, turned around, and started hitting chords to "Tombstone Blues" with this killer band. It must have been like with Jesus Christ, when the crowd threw stuff at him. I couldn't understand why they were booing him; it was the best thing I had ever heard in my life.

The Doors. I saw them in 1967 in a gymnasium at a homecoming dance, after I quit drumming. They had a big hit, "Light My Fire," so everyone thought they were going to get this romantic band. The girls showed up in their prom dresses and there were maybe twenty-five of us young derelicts who weren't in college trying to soak up whatever music we could. First, the band came out—this was their first tour and they looked untogether with a capital *U*; then out comes Morrison. He looked like Hedy Lamarr in *Samson and Delilah*. Greased, shiny black hair down to his crotch, pearl white skin, black suede Beatles-type boots, leatherette trousers, conch belt, leather jacket, and a Pete Townshend shirt with ruffles. I was transfixed with how beautiful he was. He was obviously on something. He did his best imitations of a drunk, careening around the stage. This pissed the audience, but I was in ecstasy. Deep down he was doing something I knew I could do; you didn't have to play a guitar, sing, or do anything to do that. Plus, there's this really horny young girl with a French last name swaying in front of me to the music and I'm rubbing my dick against her butt until finally I came in my pants.

HOW I LOST MY VIRGINITY

I was a virgin until I was twenty, after I had started the Stooges. There was this girl, twenty-five years old with a kid; some guy knocked her up and dumped her. She took a shine to me and I'd go over to her place when I wanted dinner, a sandwich, a beer, or a clean bed to sleep in—you know, things that girls had—and I would make out with her. One night she got me stoned on pot and she just did it to me, which pissed me off, because I didn't control the situation. But the next day I thought, I want to try some more of this.

BIG INFLUENCES

Jim Morrison's voice on the first Doors album. He was the first person I'm aware of to sing rock 'n' roll with a full baritone; up until then, if you didn't have a high voice, you would sing in a monotone,

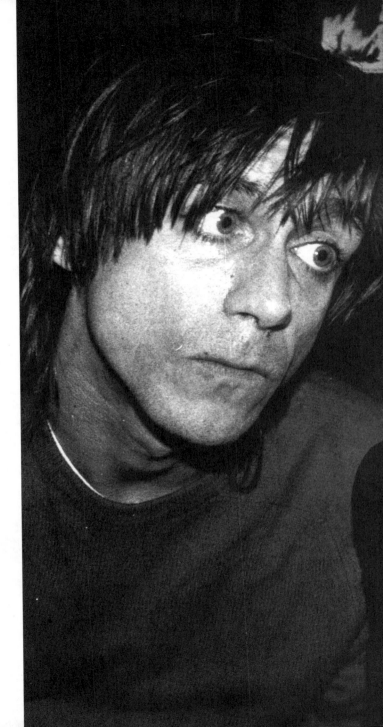

the way Mick Jagger did on *12x5*, or you shout the song, the way Bo Diddley did. Morrison sounded almost as if he were crooning, yet the background was anything but sedate.

Bo Diddley was helpful for the call-and-response; I used to use that format with great effect, without having any words planned, in the original Stooges shows.

Chuck Berry was real helpful in the way he'd look around the culture, find a catch phrase, like "sweet little sixteen," or "no particular place to go" where he talks about seat belts; he'd find neat little things in the culture on which to hang a song.

Bob Dylan *(Bringing It All Back Home* and *Highway 61 Revisited)* and Lou Reed (the banana album) both influenced me by the way they used breathy vocals and very effortlessly rode a strong beat beneath it. To me that music sounded like a bunch of Tartar tribesmen sweeping along the desert on their ponies, ready to bring savage visitation to all in their path, yet the vocals almost floating over that. I used that technique on "I Wanna Be Your dog" and "Real Cool Time."

12x5, by the Rolling Stones, for its understatement of any emotional content. There are emotions in the music, but they're kept in their place.

Frank Sinatra's "September of My Years" above all other songs, for the ability to carry the emotions in a song and to get a rise out of me, as a listener, on an emotional level. I feel something strong when that man sings.

Van Morrison (Them's first album) was a very powerful influence for the wedding of poetry and music and for the way he'd recycle blues cliche`s, like on "One-Two Brown Eyes."

Sun Ra, for his ability to use music to take you voyaging; also John Coltrane for that matter—those records opened me up.

Tina Turner, not musically because I'm not a blues shouter, nor do I have a falsetto or a hot scream, but for her stage presentation, the way she never breaks form, almost like a Balinese dancer, the hands are up, palms are outward, the feet are always going, and the tension and posture are always maintained.

SOME RECORDS YOU WOULDN'T THINK I LISTEN TO (BUT DO)

Frank Sinatra's *Only the Lonely*. It's all lonesome songs like "Lonesome Old Town," and "A Quarter to Three."

Julie London. I've got about eight of her albums

Karen Carpenter. For some reason I've been craving to cover one of her songs, "Close to You."

SOME OTHER SONGS I'D LIKE TO COVER

"September of My Years," Frank Sinatra
"96 Tears," ? and the Mysterians
"From Here to Eternity," Birthday Party
Chimes of Freedom," Bob Dylan

THREE PLACES I'D LIKE TO YODEL

Hollywood Boulevard
Beverly Center
Mt. Rushmore

SOME THINGS I'VE BEEN HIT WITH ON STAGE

Grapefruit
Beer cans
Eggs
Spit
Money
Lit cigarette butts
Mandies
Quaaludes
Joints
Bras
Panties
A fist, after playing a gig at the Rock 'n' Roll Farm in Wayne, Michigan, in the late 1970s, owned by a six-foot-five mountain man

THE BEST CURE FOR THE BLAHS

Whenever a problem has peaked and my thinking isn't getting me anywhere, I like to pull out the vacuum cleaner and vacuum the house. We've got a Singer, which we bought at the central Singer Sewing Center of the United States, up at Rockefeller Center, in New York. A sweet, little old lady sold it to us. We took pains to try out each model. It was one of the first things my wife and I bought together upon moving to New York. It was hard to get a cab, so we dragged it home. I like stroking the floor with it. In fact,

I especially like it because I'm really into rugs. I don't buy really expensive ones, but I got one with a motif of an Indian hunting deer and tigers. That's my favorite rug and I vacuum it almost religiously. I got one chair in my home; basically all my seating is within eighteen inches off the floor, so I use the rug a lot. It's almost my flying carpet. It's my thinking rug, my play rug, and a lot of times it's my kitchen table.

A WOMAN I'D LIKE TO BE

Catherine Deneuve—She plays her cards the best, looks great, doesn't give too much away, and has never been to the Betty Ford Clinic.

MY FAVORITE RIDE AT DISNEYLAND

It's A Small World—Nothing happens.

MY SECRET AMBITION

To be a member of the middle class. There's a certain mercantile definition of safety and a favorable position to which one aspires, and once you're there, at the goal line, you're happy to go around that spiral again. I know a lot of people like that, but they ain't artists; they don't live with my compulsion. I'm compelled to face myself in the morning. Call it living in the stream of living things. My work comes first; not what I can get out of it. I'm not trying to run down to the river with a bucket and see how much water I can get out of it to put in my little tub. From time to time I've even been sucked in, like everybody else, by this terrible pressure in our society to have fun and be ecstatic. If you buy a Ford, you're going to turn into a cougar and jump on top of a billboard and screw the girl in the black velvet dress. You're going to do zero to sixty in five seconds and everybody's going to ask, Who was that four-wheeled man? In our daydreams we all think we're Superman. Rock singers are nothing but low-grade forms of Superman. We're nothing but a bunch of trash Supermen. I want to get more down to earth. I like the earth. It's a fun place.

THE PART OF MY BODY THAT WOULD LOOK BEST ON PEPA
Salt:
My butt

A PART OF SALT I WISH I HAD
Pepa:
Her hair

THE BODY PART I'M PROUDEST OF
Pepa:
My chest—you can't go wrong with that.
Salt:
My Butt.

FAVORITE DESIGNER
Pepa:
Gianni Versace, maybe because he's so expensive.
Salt:
His stuff is totally overpriced.

HOW I'D DRESS SALT
Pepa:
In a hot mama outfit—something real sexy, something bold, like something you got to have nerve to wear. Something that if she wore you'd say "Oh my God, she didn't put that on." I could wear that.

SOMEONE I'D LIKE TO UNDRESS
Pepa:
Treach from Naughty by Nature

WHAT LOOKS SEXY ON ME
Salt:
Some really short shorts—not so my cheeks are hanging out
Some platform shoes, the bulky kind that they're wearing now
A leotard top with a low neck and long sleeves

HOW I'D DRESS IF I WERE BEING PHOTOGRAPHED FOR POSTERITY
Pepa:
I'd be laying down on my back, one leg up, with something light, like chiffon, that's see-through but not see-through, draped around me, as if I'm at home, it's hot, and it's raining out.

Salt:
I'd be wearing my workout clothes—Doc Martin combat boots, a leotard, and big, baggy shorts, watching "Martin" on television in the kitchen.

WHO GETS MORE DATES
Pepa:
Put it like this, I look more like I'm going to a party, so I'm the one the guy will most likely come up to. It's all in the eyes and my eyes say party. Salt's eye'll say she's having a good time, but she's not concentrating on it. For her, a guy has to be interested in her. See, I won't know because I'll just invite him anyway.

SOMEONE I ALWAYS WANTED TO MEET THAT I WISH I HADN'T
Pepa:
Whoopi Goldberg. I still like her, but the crazy's not on like before. Maybe she was just having a rough day, that's the only thing I will look at. I seen her one time and I was like "Hi" and she didn't my hi back.
Salt:
Janet Jackson. She invited us to her house once. I knew she was shy, but she was painfully shy. She's so fiery on stage, I just hoped she was more like that in person.

SOMEONE I DIDN'T WANT TO MEET BUT I'M GLAD I DID
Pepa:
I have to say Treach from Naughty by Nature. I thought he's so rough and crazy, but he's real nice.
Salt:
Arsenio Hall. I thought he would be snobbish.

FIRST POP STAR I WANTED TO GET NEXT TO
Pepa:
Eddie Murphy. He was just so rough. He was out spoken and the subjects that he attacked was reality. I thought we could communicate if I was to go out on a date with him.

Salt:
Michael Jackson—He was practically the only young, black entertainer that there was at the time I was around eight years old.

WHAT'S SEXY IN A GUY
Pepa:
Bowl legs,
a personality that's sensitive—
to me, not to the street—
and flattery
Salt:
Brown skin guys,
not over-built or skinny guys;
quiet guys,
not loud, boisterous show-offs.
The ultimate guy is the guy who knows God.

HOW TO LET A GUY DOWN EASY
Pepa:
I just get on his nerves by doing all the things he don't like until he wants to let me down.
Salt:
I lie. I've say my life is too confusing right now and I'm not going to be good for you. Anything but "I really don't like you." That would hurt me the most if someone I really liked told me that.

THE HARDEST I'VE BEEN LET DOWN
Pepa:
That only happened one time, and one time only. I caught him messing around with someone else, so he let me know his interests were no longer with me.That's cold.
Salt:
I've got cheated on and lied to. The worst is finding out everything about a person was a lie.

SOMEONE I'D LIKE TO BE FOR A MOMENT
Pepa:
The imposter going around being me. It's been going on for three years and it gets on my nerve. I want to know why this person is doing this. It's a girl with a guy who pretends to be my brother. This person knows a lot of little stuff about me and acts crazy to everybody. She gets a hold of all these stars and it's really embarrassing. Guys will come up to me, like, "What's up with me and you?" They have the wrong girl.

Salt:
Michael Jackson. There' a lot of pain and confusion going on in his head and I'd like to know what's really up with him.

A MAN I'D LIKE TO BE
Pepa:
Eddie Murphy. Eddie Murphy's crazy. Eddie Murphy's rough. Definitely Eddie Murphy in his movie *Raw*.

SOMETHING I"D LIKE TO EXPERIENCE IF I COULD BE WHITE
Salt:
I want to know why white people like to do the craziest things, like jumping out of airplanes and climbing mountains. Not so many black people do stuff like that.
Pepa:
To be president

HOW I'D DECORATE THE WHITE HOUSE
Salt:
I don't know what it looks like now but it's probably very traditional, very antiquey, and very boring. I would probably knock down a lot of walls, put in a lot of skylights mint green furniture, plenty of TVs, a full, 24-track recording studio in the basement, a workout room, and lots of mirrors.

SONGS I LOVE THAT NO ONE WOULD EXPECT ME TO
Salt:
"To Sir With Love"
Pepa:
"Back In Black" by AC/DC

RECORDS I'D GRAB IF THE HOUSE WAS ON FIRE
Salt:
"I'll Take You There," the Staples,
Bring the Boys Home," Mavis Staples
"Clean Up Woman"
Pepa:
"Under New Management," Miki Howard
"Nothing Compares 2 U," Sinead O'Connor

A HOUSEHOLD PRODUCT I'D LIKE TO HAVE MY PICTURE ON
Pepa:
Sugar Pops
Salt:
Lifestyle condoms—lubricated

SIT-COM WE WISH WE WERE ON
"Martin"

FIRST EXPENSIVE THING I BOUGHT FOR MYSELF
Pepa:
A BMW 525i; it was the style out at the time. And I went shopping at all the expensive stores in Beverly Hills, where a little scarf costs $1000.
Salt:
A Porche 911 that I don't drive, that I wish I hadn't bought, that I totaled and I shouldn't have even fixed. I bought it because it's a status symbol but I have a plain old Nissan Pathfinder that's three years old and it's always dirty and that's what I drive every day.

MOST VALUED POSSESSION
Pepa:
A tennis necklace. You know how they have a tennis bracelet—big diamonds that go all the way around? Well, I have a tennis necklace.
Salt:
My daughter's crib

WHO PICKS UP THE CHECK AT RESTAURANTS
Salt:
I will grab it and say this is my treat more times than she.
Pepa:
It's even to the penny. She owes me $2.50 right now and I'll get it back the next time we go out.

THE FURTHEST I'VE GONE FOR KICKS
Pepa:
Bungi jumping—backwards. The bungi I jumped off was 250 feet in the air. It was on a crane in Daytona Beach and the birds were flying below me. Now I want to jump out of a plane.
Salt:
Skinny dipping in the Virgin Islands with my cousins— all girl cousins—on a real dark night

SOME PLACE I'D LIKE TO YODEL
Pepa:
In Switzerland—somewhere where I won't look stupid
Salt:
In the Senate, during one of those real boring sessions where they're pretending they care about something

SOMEONE I'D LIKE TO BE THE PARENT OF
Pepa:
Michael Jordan
Salt:
Madonna—somebody who is troubled

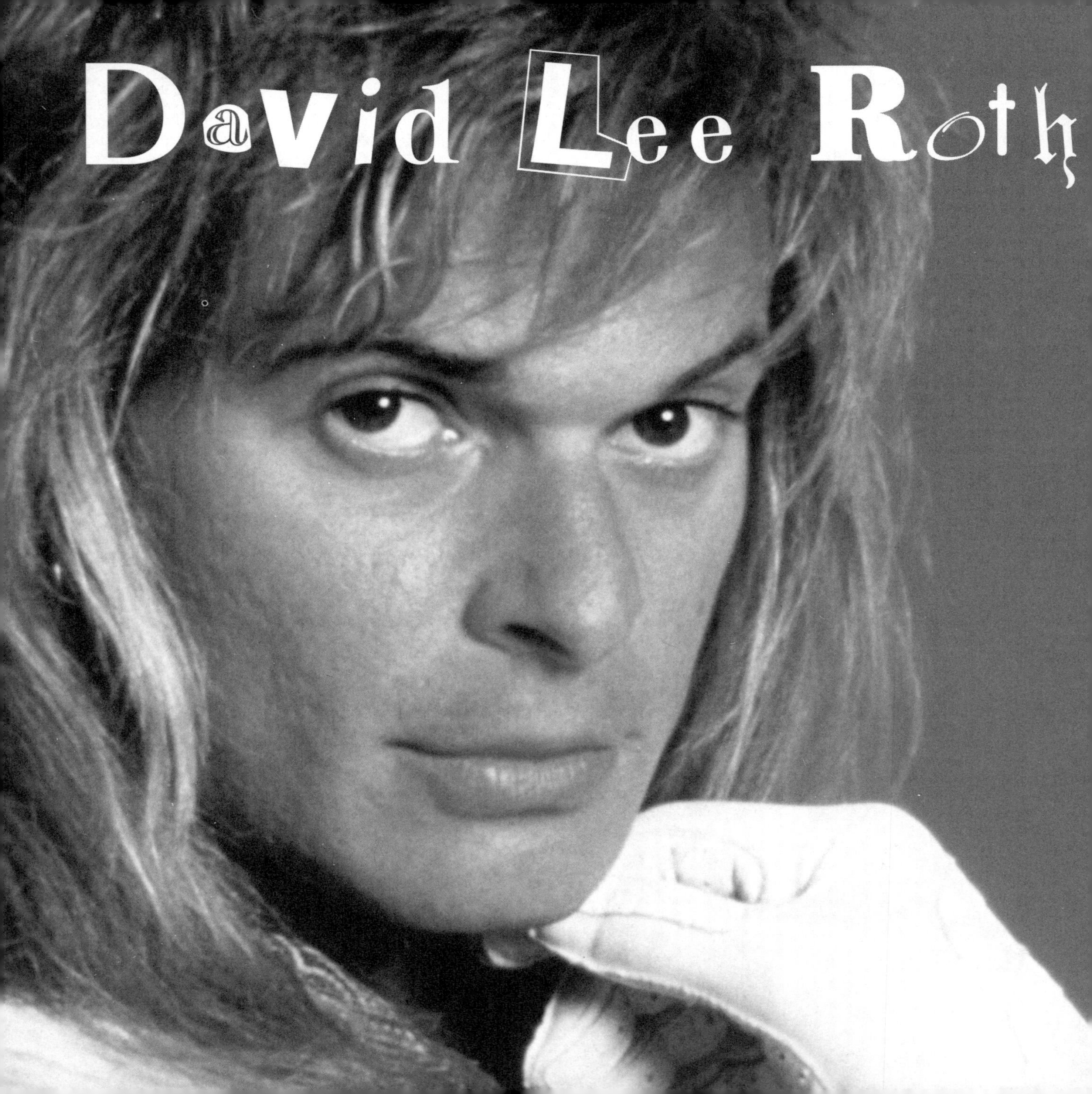
David Lee Roth

AN ALBUM COVER I WISH I WAS ON
Victoria at Sea-- when the tower exploded and the smoke is bruised purple and heading skyward.

A MAGAZINE I ALWAYS WANTED TO BE IN
Life, because I was always a big fan of *Life* photographs, especially the historical ones, the ones that documented a certain space in time, like one of Weegee's photos, who shot *Confidential*, or whatever it was, that capture a specific emotion. *Life* magazine finally did show up, about three, four or five years ago, and they took a picture of how shitty my hotel room looked and made a double page spread out of it, too.

A PAIR OF PANTS I WANT TO BE IN
Ones like Blue Boy was wearing in his painting.

BANDS I WISH I HAD BEEN IN
Robin Hood and his merry men. A bunch of guys in matching outfits fighting with sticks, taking from the rich, and giving to the poor. (I know you're out there thinking, "You already do that, Dave.")

A band of roving Gypsies. They were always very colorful people in that they contain the essence of magic and the ominous qualities of the forbidden that could only be passed from family to family; at least the Gypsies in the Frankenstein movies did.

The Magnificent Seven, again, a bunch of guys united under one theme song

A marching band like John Phillip Sousa—Nothing matches blowing brass when it's in full force.

A MOVIE I WISH I HAD BEEN IN
Some Like It Hot. I wish I could have been the violin case Marilyn Monroe was carrying, in the scene where she's walking alongside the train, with all the smoke and steam coming out, and the way she looked. Did you ever try to make your eyes like that? Millions of people have tried to make their eyes like that and she probably didn't try at all.

A BED I WISH I COULD HAVE BEEN IN
I certainly don't wish I could have been in it, but I wish I had Hugh Hefner's bed from the sixties. It was the first round bed you ever saw and it rotated. It had a stereo

console and the digital dialed read-out Computex, a wet bar, and we'd never seen anything like it, much less the girls in it.

A BED I'D RATHER NOT HAVE BEEN IN
I remember being in the Amazon for six and a half weeks and wishing I could have been in any bed. It was the first time in my life during a long period of applied stress that I had to deal with a hammock. Hammocks are always romanticized because you imagine people in white Panama hats sipping drinks in the torrid clubs. Actually, hammocks just bend you into the shape of a safety pin and keep you there.

UNDER MY BED
When I was five years old the foreman at the ranch back in Indiana told me that beneath my bed was the boogie man, with big teeth, huge round eyes, and a burlap sack, who put little guys who would get out of bed before morning into it and take them away. I still have a neurosis about getting out of bed before two in the afternoon.

Then there was the point in my life when *The Carpetbaggers*, by Harold Robbins, was under my mattress. What a juicy novel that was. And a big one, too. It created a hard spot to sleep on, until I took it out from under the mattress and read a chapter or two. That created an even harder spot to sleep on.

PEOPLE'S DREAMS I WISH I WERE IN

People often confuse dreams with the imagination. Dreams are things that are based more on impossibilities than likelihood. Places and people and scenarios that couldn't possibly exist. But imagination is what really gets you there. Imagination got the guy to the top of Everest without oxygen. Imagination got the person to invent the electric toothbrush. It was imagination that broke the four-minute mile. I only use physical examples because we can picture these in our mind a little more readily than people who have created intangible things like music or dances. You don't just suddenly reach a point in your life where you imagine you're going to climb Mt. Everest. You have to build up to it. You start off at some point looking to other people and what they're doing with their imagination, and after living a little bit through their visions you begin to catch the rhythm and say perhaps I can imagine a little bit on my own. That's basically what I do for a living. I never wanted to be a part of somebody else's dreams.

TEAMS IN HISTORY I WISH I HAD BEEN ON

Maurice Herzog's team, on the first assault on Anapurna, in the Himalayas. It was Herzog who wrote the definitive expedition novel, where you simply do not make it to base camp until at least page 120, and the oncoming storm season threatens to cancel the entire expedition and there's beginning to be dissension among the expert members, but one final desperate summit bid results in much frostbite and victory.

The Rocky and Mick team, in *Rocky*, where the Burgess Meredith character, Mick, his corner man, says "Listen to me, Rock, you're a very dangerous man." Everybody could use a Mick in their life at one point or another. I don't have one currently, but maybe that's my job now.

Mick Leahy and the Taylor Boys when they first went over the hill in New Guinea and encountered the fierce cannibal tribes. I guess I get that same feeling when I go over the hill into Burbank and visit Warner Brothers.

I would like to have been with Madam Curie and her husband when they discovered uranium. There's got to be a special extra something when you discover or invent something really marvelous with a soul mate. That's something I haven't done in quite awhile.

PEOPLE'S SHOES I'D LIKE TO BE IN

There are some people's shoes I would certainly like to be in while they're in them, but I would have to get much bigger shoes and get in them first. Then I'd have the next person, with their back to me, stand on my feet, which reminds me of an old story I read in a romance novel where it said, "She surrendered herself as never before in her life as a woman, and she felt his heart beating directly next to hers." That gave me pause for thought because, anatomically speaking, if his heart is beating directly next to hers, they can't be face to face. He would have to be directly behind her, which certainly makes the story brighten up a little or maybe one of them is hanging upside down, which is probably more colorful than the author had intended, but, hey, that's what poetry is all about.

PACKAGES I'D LIKE TO BE ON

A box of Trix
A bottle of Night Train
A box of Tampax

A WRONG I'D LIKE TO SEE RIGHTED

The license plate on my 1951 Mercury lowrider says "MR. WRONG."

HANKERINGS I HAVE

I got to be me.
Climb every mountain.
To ride like the wind and be free again.
(And especially) I wish they all could be California girls.

James Brown

THE DEODORANT OF THE HARDEST WORKING MAN
IN SHOW BUSINESS
Right Guard

BIGGEST INFLUENCES
Gorgeous George the wrestler
Louis Jordan
Roy Brown
Jackie Robinson
Joe Louis

THREE BANDS I'D LIKE TO HAVE PLAYED KEYBOARDS IN
Jimmy Dorsey's
Glenn Miller's
Count Basie's

WHERE THE WORDS TO "FOR GOODNESS SAKES, LOOK AT THOSE CAKES" COME FROM
God

SOMETHING I WANTED TO BE BEFORE I BECAME AN ENTERTAINER
A pitcher—I had a good fast ball, curve, and knuckler.
A boxer—2-0-1 in three professional fights

SOMEONE I WAS IN A PREVIOUS LIFETIME
Moses

FAVORITE TV SHOWS
"Nightwatch"
"David Letterman"
"Oprah"
"Dolly Parton"
"Soul Train"
"The Jeffersons"
"Gimme a Break"
"Bustin' Loose"
"60 Minutes"

HOW THE WORLD GOT FUNKY
When I wrote "Papa's Got a Brand New Bag," in
Cincinnati, 1965

THE DEFINITION OF FUNK
Funk is the root of the blues. It's soul, jazz, and gospel.
Funk is coming down on the one. If it's on the one,
it's funky. But it's hard for me to get people to understand
that. It took me four or five years to get Bootsy Collins to
understand what "on the one" was.

DEFINITION OF COOL
James Brown

DEFINITION OF HOT
James Brown
David Bowie
Mick Jagger
Charlie Pride
Johnny Cash
Roy Clark
Barbara Mandrell
Gladys Knight
Dionne Warwick
Stevie Wonder
the Supremes
Wilson Pickett—can't forget Wilson Pickett

SOME LOVES OF MY LIFE
Aretha Franklin
Tammi Terrell
Mrs. Adrienne Brown
[The third and current Mrs. James Brown, whom he met in 1982 on "Solid Gold," where she was the show's hairstylist and makeup artist and who once dated Elvis Presley]

PAPA'S BRAND NEW BAG
Is made of black vinyl and upholstery so it can be easily spotted at airports. It's a long hanging bag that can be packed faster and handled easier than luggage, although I got some new, flexible luggage, too, made of Naugahyde by a young man in Augusta by the name of Green. I got over two thousand uniforms and I'll take fifty suits on the road, plus capes, shoes and the rest, and wear something different every show. Each bag might hold up to fifteen costumes and weighs about seventy-five pounds.

THREE BRIDGES I'D LIKE TO BE TAKEN TO
The Golden Gate Bridge
The Oakland Bay Bridge
A covered bridge in Georgia near my home that I'd like my wife to see.
(We have a lot of driving to do.)

SOMETHING I NEVER GET A CHANCE TO DO
Water ski

POLITICIANS WHO'VE RETURNED MY CALLS
Mr. Reagan
Mr. Bush
Senator Thurmond
Governor Harris
Senator Sam Nunn
Senator Hubert Humphrey, my favorite politician of all time

A POLITICIAN WHO HASN'T
President Carter

THE PLACE I'D MOST LIKE TO DANCE
The Reagan White House

THE BEST FLOOR TO DANCE ON
Slate; polished wood

HOW RIVALS HAVE TRIED TO SABOTAGE ME
By making the floor rough and taking away the slide. But that don't stop me from dancing.

HOW TO DO THE JAMES BROWN
Combine the applejack, the dolo, which is a slide, almost like the skate, and the scallyhop, which is a takeoff on the lindy hop, add a nerve control technique that makes the whole body tremble, and you got the James Brown.

Young MC

WHAT GETS ME OUT OF BED IN THE MORNING
The Pet Shop Boys
New Order
Big Daddy Kane

BANDS I WISH I HAD BEEN IN
The Eagles
The Rolling Stones
Earth, Wind & Fire
Fleetwood Mac
The Fifth Dimension

MOVIES I WISH I HAD BEEN IN
Dead Poets Society
Do the Right Thing
Lethal Weapon II

RERUNS ON TV I NEVER MISS
"Sanford and Son"
"All My Children"

COURSES IN SCHOOL I DID BEST IN
Eco-381 (Statistics)
Eco-465 (Economy of Law)
Programming Data Processing 250 (Lotus and D-Base)

SOMEONE I'D LIKE TO RUB NOSES WITH
Jayne Kennedy

BEST PERK THAT COMES WITH MY JOB
Having the secretary at the record company type up my lyrics

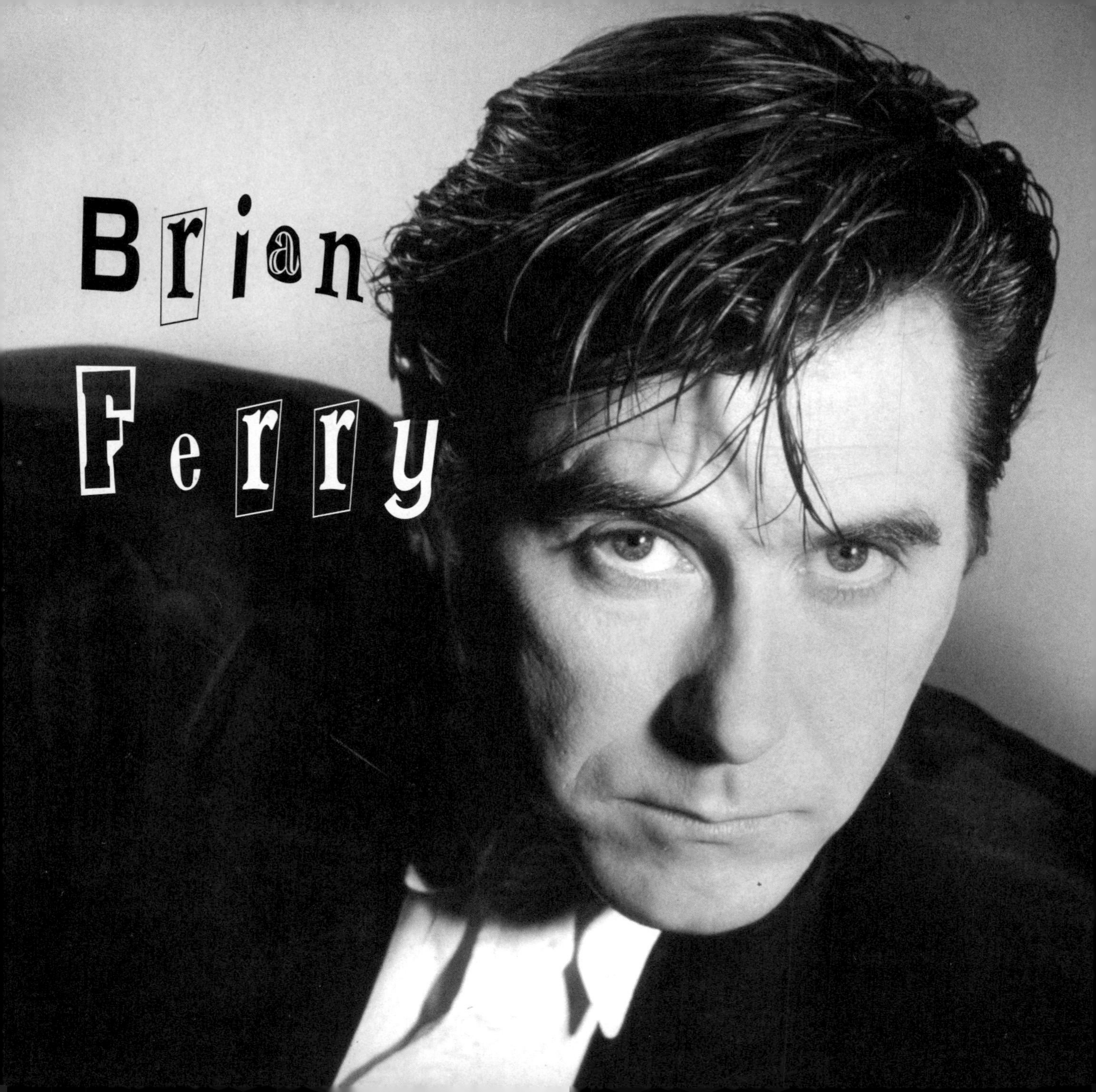
Brian
Ferry

TWO GREAT PLEASURES IN LIFE
To hear yourself on the radio
To go into some obscure place and find your record
on the juke box

WHAT I'D DO IF I WASN'T A ROCK STAR
What I was doing before; be an artist, though possibly not a
very good one

A COUPLE OF THINGS I'VE WANTED TO BE
A film star
A great academic

WHY I CHOSE ROCK 'N' ROLL
Because it chose me. It seduces people from a very early
age. I was living a dual life. At night I was playing in a
group—I had this soul band and I was kind of arranging it
and managing it—and during the day I was in a
completely different environment in art school. The group
went professional and I decided I wasn't ready to do that. I
wanted to stay on and get my degree and give myself a
chance at what I was doing. Even while I was doing art I
was very much into music and thinking in musical terms.
And when I was doing music, I thought in very graphic
terms. Even in a song I was interested in structure;
I thought in terms of shapes, like designing a building. If I
was describing to a musician what I thought, I found
it easier to draw things than to explain it. I found music
and art to be very interrelated, except I thought I was
an artist and always felt the need for an audience.

THE DIFFERENCE BETWEEN AN ARTIST AND A ROCK STAR
I tend to think they're closely related. Obviously the
practice is very different, the lifestyle is completely
different, the rewards are different. The actual
creative process is very similar; I've always found doing
anything to be very difficult. Ideas for things came easily,
but the actual execution of them was a real drag. I'd always
imagine these great paintings, but they never came out like
I had in mind.

MY FAVORITE SINGER OF ALL TIME
Billie Holiday

A FAVORITE BEAUTY OF ALL TIME
Rita Hayworth

WHAT I THINK ABOUT WHEN I SING
If it's a song that's been done before, I think about what I
can do with it; if it's something that's
dead serious, I have a sense of irony and I just know what
people will find amusing.
I can sing the most banal lyrics and kind of believe them
and also feel that this song is going to be camp.
Or I put myself in the situation of a teenager and how it felt
to me when I first heard the song.

MY FAVORITE FASHION
The more severe looks that come out of Paris
Tacky high fashion

WHERE I GET MY FASHION SENSE
I worked in a tailor's when I was at school, where I first became interested in clothes. I like clothes but I don't like to get dressed up all the time. I sort of like to play out roles.

A ROLE MODEL
Elmore James—He was incredibly shy and always sang with his back toward the audience.

SOMETHING I'M A SUCKER FOR
Anything to do with beaches or the sea

MY IDEA OF A DREAM DATE
A blind date. That would have an edge. Or with someone you knew a bit about but hadn't actually spoken to before, so you had something to think about before you went out. And there's nothing wrong with good food. You can always start out going to a good restaurant, preferably with just a few other people, intimates, just so you can bounce off a few corners and you don't have any of these " ho-hum" sort of things. Then, after you've eaten at Maxim's, if you are in Paris, or Mirabelle in London, you could go to one of the clubs and then to one of the other clubs. Gradually the party would whittle down and then, um, I don't know. Sometimes it's nice to finish off gambling, as long as the stakes aren't too high. I hate losing. Actually, an ideal date on a cruise ship would be nice. Then you'd have all those walking-the-deck routines. You can have a lot of fun in the tackiest clubs if you're with the right people. I'm just as much a fan of low life as I am of the high. It's just the horrible in-between things that I can't get into.

WHAT BORES ME MOST
Decadence and being associated with it. I like to live as varied a life as possible and not be considered one thing or another. Decadence always seemed applied to people who adopted nouveau-sleeziness and wore drag makeup.

Ru Paul

AN ALBUM COVER I WISH WAS MINE
Cher's *Take Me Home*. It's the one where she's lit like a futuristic Viking woman. It's so blurry, retouched to filth. It's my favorite kind of photography and my favorite cover of all time.

RECORDS YOU WOULDN'T THINK I LIKE TO BUT DO
Paula Abdul, *Vibeology*
Hank Williams, Jr., *Honky Tonking*
Anything by Olivia Newton-John

FIVE TEENAGE CRUSHES
David Bowie—He really touched me, musically and on other levels. I fell for him and wrote "Bowie" everywhere.

Amy Stewart—She sang "Knock on Wood," a number one disco hit.

Bette Midler—because she's outrageous and her clothes have a great sense of humor about them.

Grace Jones—of course

Cher—My sister told me Cher never wore a dress and I've been a Cher fan ever since.

SITCOMS THAT INFLUENCED ME
"The Jeffersons"
"Good Times"
"The Carol Burnette Show"
Most of all, the "Cher" show and the variety shows of the '70s—that's my idea of what show business is all about: seamless, gorgeous, well-lit, beautiful music and funny schtick.

MY IDEA OF HOLLYWOOD GOOD-LOOKING
Mathew Modine—I like long legs, I like lean, love a big gorgeous nose and bright eyes.

FIRST EXPENSIVE THING I BOUGHT
A lace front wig—a custom made wig that looks like the hair is coming out of your scalp

MY HEIGHT IN STOCKING FEET
6' 4 1/2"

WITH A WIG

It varies, depending upon how tall my hair is, how big my attitude is. Stick a wig on Michael Jordan—
that's how tall I am.

WHAT I LOOK FOR IN A WIG

I like a blond wig right now, because I'm embarking upon world domination and the world responds to blond hair. If I have one life to live, let me live it as a blond. But I need a lot of hair because my hairstyles require lots of volume, so I like a wig with a lot of hair at the dome of the head.

WHAT I LOOK FOR IN A PAIR OF FALSIES

There's only one kind—foam. For a long time I'd stick in there whatever I could get my hands on, but at least modern bras have a wide selection of sizes. I like an A cup. It fits my build best because I have wide shoulders. A B would be too much. But when I wear a pushup bra, I'll wear a 34C. Getting a pushup bra really turned my life around. It's an amazing item because you don't even have to have anything on your chest to effect cleavage; you even fool yourself.

HOW I'D DESCRIBE MYSELF TO SOMEONE MEETING ME AT AN AIRPORT

I'm the tall Black man with the shaved head, and if you get closer, I have freckles. I'd be wearing some khaki pants, a pocket T-shirt, and Birkenstocks.

PHASES I'VE GONE THROUGH

Fun, happy, androgynous sailor. That was my first persona.

My jungle period, where I wore a Mohawk, G-string, and wadding boots

My Road Warrior look, where my Mohawk got bigger and taller, and I wore shoulder pads, a jock strap, and high heel candy pumps

Grunge drag look combat boots, with a mini skirt, no stockings, some halter top with no titties, and either my Mohawk or a ratty wig

A go-go dancer, where I had every look you can imagine

Abstract drag, where I was an echo

For the past two and a half years I've been doing my goddess drag, which is the biggest hair, the tallest shoes, the tinest waist.

TIME IT TAKES ME TO TRANSFORM MYSELF

About three hours—and fifteen minutes to transform back.

MY FAVORITE FLOAT IN THE THANKSGIVING DAY PARADE

Spiderman; and of course Bugs Bunny, the ultimate drag queen, the ultimate heckler.

PLACES I'VE BEEN A FIXTURE AT

The Pyramid Club. I still go there.
The Film Forum movie theater
Mega Fitness, where I work out four days a week
Patricia Fields Boutique. I have to go in there at least twice a week; they supply me with my pushup bras and tuck-in panties.

MY FAVORITE ERA IN FASHION

The '70s. I love colors, I love textures, and I love wild silhouettes. It's when fashion went on vacation and came back to find the house had been raided. That had been a piss take on everything we had held dear to our hearts up until that point.

THREE GURUS I'D MOST LIKE TO HANG OUT WITH

Berry Gordy
Karl Larggerfelf
Barry Gibbs (maybe)

PLACE I'D MOST LIKE TO HANG OUT IN

Joan Rivers' living room

FAVORITE THRIFT STORE

Patricia Fields. You can go in there with very little money and come out with more than a look—a personality, Yourself, and a side order of fries.

SOMETHING I ALWAYS SAY

You're born naked and the rest is drag.

A GOWN I'D MOST LIKE TO DIRECT TRAFFIC IN

A Versace creation gown. I'd be at the intersection of 59th and Fifth, outside the Plaza Hotel.

Laurie AnderSon

BANDS I WISH I HAD BEEN IN

The house band that played ice skating music at the Coliseum while the Christians were being killed

A band of angels with telescopes

One of the pickup bands Elvis had around the pool in his later movies

THREE PEOPLE ON MY BEST-DRESSED LIST

Any one of the girls wearing a short tight skirt, puffy sleeves, and boots while hanging around Elvis's pool

Janet Munnecke —When I grew up in Glen Ellyn, Illinois, we had a clash club, where we wore clothes that clashed, like stripes and plaids and polka dots, and Janet's clothes clashed the best.

Junior Walker, who wore processed hair and shiny suits

A TEAM I WISH I COULD BE ON

The Olympic Synchronized Swimming team. I'd like to play the fifth petal in the flower pattern.

SOMETHING I LOST AND NEVER FOUND

A zebra skin rug. That was on my floor and then somehow I lost it while moving from one place to another. It went with my zebra skin bongo drums, zebra skin purse, and zebra skin headband outfit.

FIVE MEN I'D LIKE TO DATE (AT ONCE)

Dan Quayle
Ted Mooney (the writer)
Wuddo Occkels
Two of his fellow Dutch astronauts

THINGS THAT HAVE INFLUENCED MY MUSIC

William Burroughs's voice, hat, and briefcase
Captain Beefheart's visions
Opossum with red-eye gravy

MY FAVORITE RECIPE FOR HOTEL HOT DOGS

Pick up a couple of hot dogs on your way back to your hotel. Cut the lamp cord with a knife, strip the wire down with wire strippers, thread the wire through the hot dogs and plug it in, letting the drippings fall onto the rug. Cooking time is a couple of seconds with 220 volts, four seconds with 110 volts.

A MOVIE I'D LIKE TO SEE RIGHT NOW
The Toxic Avenger

THE BEST BED I EVER SLEPT IN

The one with eight hundred pillows in the Moroccan theme room of this hotel in London. The night I was there, John Denver was in the Tokyo theme room.

SOMEONE'S SHOES I WOULDN'T MIND BEING IN

The game warden's at the fish hatchery in New Mexico where I was at recently. They're brown boots with treaded soles that look very comfortable. I also loved his navy blue uniform with fish and game warden patches on the sleeves. The smell reminded me of Canada, with lakes, little motor boats, and wooden docks. It was the freshest, sweetest smell. The game warden said they had a job opening; all I needed was a high school diploma, which I have.

SONGS THAT MAKE ME WANT TO HAVE SEX

"Happy Birthday," by Marilyn Monroe
"The Ten Commandments of Love," by Princess Buster

SOMEONE I'M DYING TO INTERVIEW
Nancy Reagan. I'm very curious how someone who wears
a size four survives.

A CROWD IN HISTORY I'D LIKE TO HAVE BEEN PART OF
One of the Indian tribes ice skating on bearskins while
playing hockey in Minnesota

THE DEFINITION OF HEAVEN
A place where you don't have to lock your door

MY FOUR BIGGEST FEARS
Being really deep underwater
Sharks
Darkness
Claustrophobia

TWO PEOPLE I'D LIKE TO BE THE MOTHER OF
Johnny and Edgar Winters

B r i a n

W i l s o n

WHERE I WENT WHEN I WENT INTO SECLUSION

To my room. I stayed there for four years.

WHY I WENT THERE

Because I ran out of ideas and I just got zapped. I had personal problems that totally zapped me, that took three or four years to recover from. That's where I got the stomach. I laid around and got fat.

WHAT I DID IN MY ROOM FOR FOUR YEARS

Beat off. Watched TV. I didn't read. I couldn't see, my eyes are too bad. I could have gotten a pair of glasses. That would have helped me. I stayed in my room and wouldn't see anyone. I reclused it, definitely. I don't know how, but I somehow got into weird stuff in my head. All mind and no activity.

HOW IT FELT TO BE A RECLUSE

Pretty powerful. I felt power, but I didn't know what it was about. I couldn't relate it to anything. I felt a power, but what the hell's a power if you don't know what it was. Maybe it wasn't my power. I could have been feeling somebody else's. A lot of time I feel my music belongs to someone else.

WHEN I HAD THIS FEELING BEFORE

When we did "Surfer Girl" there was a mystical thing that happened that night that I can't describe; all I can tell you is that it was beyond anything I had known before. "Surfer Girl" symbolized a mystical place that I have never been to but sung about. Maybe I was there, I don't know. I could have been and not known it.

WHY I WENT INTO SECLUSION

We went to Holland and left town. We left all our friends and when we came back there was a really weird vibe. I got into some really weird relationships and more and more piled up and pretty soon I was locked away in that God damn room. And you know, there was nothing I could do. First, I went through this shit where I'd say I don't know a God damn thing about making commercial records. So I went through this thing about trying to find out what that commercial formula was and I finally said fuck it, the Beach Boys don't amount to shit and aren't part of that business anymore.

LITTLE DEUCE COUPE· SURFER GIRL · CATCH
IN MY ROOM · THE ROCKING SURFER · SURFER'S RU

IRL
EACH BOYS

Capitol RECORDS

HIGH FIDELITY

- THE SURFER MOON • SOUTH BAY SURFER • HAWAII
CAR CLUB • YOUR SUMMER DREAM • BOOGIE WOODIE

WHY WE WENT TO HOLLAND
We had a studio in our house and my wife decided to pull it out—that was in 1972—and all the guys said, fuck it, we're going to go to Holland and build a studio there. We went for about half a year and when we came back, everything fucking went up in smoke. We were so fucking out of touch. At that time it was really hard and then, finally, I don't know what happened.

WHAT REALLY HAPPENED
I took acid. That's what I was experiencing: an overload of programing. I figured the only way to deal with that was to say fuck everything rather than to deal with anything. In other words, it was a natural circuit switch. I couldn't understand why it would happen to me.
And pretty soon I was locked away in that God damn room. I couldn't understand until finally I got so low that there was room enough for me to start soaking in only what I wanted. This was the last part of '72, '73, '74, '75, and it was just at the top of '76 that I started to snap back.

SOMETHING I WASN'T GETTING ENOUGH OF
Health foods. I should have gotten more of those.

SOMETHING I GOT TOO MUCH OF
The sex. I was overdoing the sex. It zapped my energy and I didn't know what to do about it. I really like sex. I can do it all the time. There's no way to stop it.

MY BIGGEST FEAR
Losing the Beach Boys, or having the Beach Boys bomb. I wouldn't have had shit. No money coming in, nothing.

HOW TO KEEP IN CONTROL
It's a matter of mental and physical purity, which we underestimate. They say you are what you eat. It's hard to assimilate that statement because you can go, "Okay, I drink a lot of beer, so I must be a big bottle of beer," but no, actually it's true. If you take a lot of speed, you become that way. If you take a lot of vitamins and good food, you start grooving. Which is hard to do. It's a hard discipline. You go sit there in the kitchen and look at those bottles. You go gulp, gulp, gulp. You got to force them down. You got to do it.

THE TOUGHEST THING ABOUT BEING A BEACH BOY

Having to go on TV or on stage to perform. I have the hangup of thinking I wouldn't be able to go on television and really handle it. I couldn't handle people watching me talk. I admit that I make up for my lack of confidence by writing music. I pass on this, pass on that, cop out on this, run away from that, go right to the piano and make up for it. I'd quit this business altogether if I figured I couldn't sing.

SOMETHING ELSE I COPPED OUT ON

Writing songs. I run away from it. That's another hangup I go through.

WHERE MY SONGS COME FROM

Now and then, ideas for songs seem to come from heaven and from other places I don't know where the heck they were. Melodies and stuff would come from heaven. The melodies start happening first and the words come after.

SOME GREAT SONG WRITERS

Burt Bacharach
Paul McCartney

HOW I BECAME A BEACH BOY

Through my brother Dennis. He said, "Hey, we got to write a song about surfing. All the kids at school would like it." My brothers and Mike Love helped me a little bit on the lyrics. We were just thinking about trying to get a fad going; we weren't thinking so much of the sport. I wasn't into that surfing stuff. I didn't care. I never tried it. Even when we got further along I didn't know a thing about it, but it seemed right, it really did. I'd seen a lot of movies. I saw Endless Summer and it turned me on. I saw how it looked and I saw the the whole culture and I identified, I pretended like I was really into it, which I wasn't. Same with cars. I learned a lot from my brother, went to a lot of hamburger stands, got into it.

MY FIRST CARS

'51 Mercury, which I had for two years
Then a '57 Ford
Then a red '60 Chevy
Then a Porche
Jaguar
Cadillac
Rolls Royce
Corvette
Station wagon

SOMETHING I WOULD HAVE DONE IF I DIDN'T END UP IN ROCK 'N' ROLL

I was all set to go into baseball. I thought I would be a major league player. I was the centerfielder on my high school team.

THE BIGGEST INFLUENCE ON MY GAME

Mickey Mantle

MY LIFETIME BATTING AVERAGE

I had a shitty average—169. I struck out all the time. But I felt I was a good player.

MY FAVORITE TV SHOW WHEN I WAS A KID

"Ozzie and Harriet"

HOW I GOT OUT OF THE ARMY

On a deaf ear and bedwetting

WHY I PUT A SANDBOX BENEATH MY PIANO

For inspiration, as though I was at the beach. I wanted to feel what I was doing. I wanted to run my toes through the sand while I played.

WHY I PUT A TENT IN MY LIVING ROOM

To write. It was a twelve-by-four-foot Arabian tent I put up when we lived in Beverly Hills. I wrote a lot with Van Dyke Parks in that tent. But there was no air in the fucking thing so I had to take it down.

MY FAVORITE BEACH BOYS SONGS

"Surfer Girl." That's my favorite. I was going with a girl named Judy at the time and I wrote it about her.

"Surf's Up." That was done at a particular time. Who knows what drugs I was on? I was kind of zapped.

"Fun, Fun, Fun." That was written on a freeway when I was going to San Bernadino, to a show. I was tapping on the steering wheel when I wrote the damn melody. Then when we were in Australia, Mike and I wrote the song.

"California Girls." I wanted to write about girls. At first I was going to call the song "Yeah, I Dig the Girls," like it says in the fadeout.

"Busy Doin' Nothing." That's my favorite song.

"Good Vibrations." That one took us about three months, about five recording studios and $16,000. We spliced it from the different recording studios, I call "Good Vibrations" a rock symphony, written as a symphony, not a song. The first version was a straight R&B version.

A SONG I NEVER SHOULD HAVE DONE
'"Fire." Then there was a fire so we junked it. It spooked me out. It was the wrong move, we shouldn't have done the song. It had a lot of violence, screeching, and a lot of weird, howling noises.

HOW I WANT TO LOOK IN MY STILL LIFE
Wearing jeans and no shirt, no shoes, looking as though I was getting some exercise.

SOMETHING I CAN'T LIVE WITHOUT
My vitamins, my herbs, my ginseng. I can't do without my ginseng.

SOMETHING MORE BEAUTIFUL THAN A TWENTY-FOOT WAVE
A twenty-one-foot wave

RuN

DEFINITION OF OLD SCHOOL
Kurtis Blow

Cheeba, Starski—They're Old School.

Public Enemy would be considered Old School. When they stepped in, they felt like a group that was down.

When you say Mick Jagger, you definitely say Old School

DEFINITION OF DEF
Def is cool.
It's an all around feeling that you give off,
that you keep with you.
Heavy D is def—he's incredible.
JVCs used to be def—they were the coolest boxes.
But boom boxes aren't important anymore.
It's more important to have a system in your car.
Nobody wants to carry a big, heavy tape recorder.
Now it's a Benz with a kit,
a BMW with a kit-skirt,
spoilers,
mirror wheels,
tinted windows,
a wing and a system.
Old School is def—
the guys who've been getting down and been rapping
long ago and really got in there
like DJ Hollywood, who was rapping
before there was such a thing as rap records.

WHERE I FIT IN
People don't know but I'm real Old School.   Run, he's from way back.
I was Son of Kurtis Blow. I would hook up his equipment. Then I split off
from Kurt when I was sixteen and picked up my group. I put down DMC and I
put down Jam Master J because I had the feeling that I was going to
be large. I was always a spotlight person. I would do shows when Kurt had
records out. That would already have me on the rise in my
neighborhood. So when I was thinking about my first record, I expected to be
in there, but I was worried about being in there alone. I didn't want
to do it without any homeboys.

DEFINITION OF COOL
The way Jam Master J plays our group. He's out there with the R&B and all the new stuff going on. And DMC. He's just like the real B-boy who won't take his Addidas off. He's got that patented face like Alfred E. Newman. And me, I consider myself to be completely crazy, dusted out of my brain, never know what I'm going to say.

SOMETHING DEF TO SAMPLE
"Mary, Mary," by the Monkees

DEFINITION OF NEW SCHOOL
Hightop fades,
R&B,
dance steps—that's New School.
The New School guys coming up don't compare to Old School, though they're cool in their own way. New School rappers are just learning about rap. Some guys say "I'm Old School, I just wasn't down." Well, that's what makes you New School—because you're just getting down.
New School samples James Brown too much.
It was a bad record that Chuck D made, "Rebel Without a Pause." It was so bad that everybody tried to duplicate it. He wasn't the first to sample James Brown, but he was the first to do it and seriously kill with it.

DEFINITION OF UNCOOL
L.L. Cool J.
He's good on the mike, but I don't like his records. I look for coolness in an M.C.

Big Daddy Kane gives off a cool image, but as far as L.L. goes, he's anything but cool. He's a great poet, his rhymes are good, he makes sense, and he can tell a hell of a story but he's just not that def to me no more.

James Brown for sampling, as far as I'm concerned. I can't mess with him and I don't think anyone else should. They shouldn't be sampling him so much because it makes the shit get corny

RECORDS THAT MATTERED

"Will You Still Love Me Tomorrow?" It was my song, my bowling alley, make-out-in-the-dark song.

"Scratchy," by Travis Wammic. When I heard that I traded in my Roy Orbison, Fabian, and Everly Brothers.

The first Stones album, the Who, the Rats, and of course the Pretty Things—the guys with the hair down the back, and the boots. That look still knocks me out.

SOME CLASSICS

The Beach Boys' *Smiley Smile*. That album is so heavy, it's right off the shelf. It's easy to understand, and then again, it's so fucking out there, like Andy Warhol; how simple to take a can of soup and blow it up, but he was the first person to do it, and it was genius. Brian Wilson did that too. He took real obvious stuff and did it so well. I mean, "My Favorite Vegetables," that's big-time for me.

John Steinbeck's *Travels with Charley*

Martin Scorcese's *Mean Streets*

Rodan—The scene with the eggs and the little baby at the end made me cry.

Dave Clark Five's turtle neck shirts

The Beatles boot with the high heel and the pointy toe

The Florsheim boot in 1968 that came up to the calf and had the longest heel—I must have gone through eight pairs of those, because every time I found a fox, she'd want my boots and I'd wind up giving them to her, so she would walk all over me with them.

The classic Mercedes 210, eggshell with red leather interior, and the Porsche turbo Carrera

Photographs of groups of people on the beach at Coney Island, opium dens, and the stuff by that artist who took a couch and brought it all over the world

Anything Hawaiian

THREE GREAT TRICKSTERS

Elvis. He never wrote any songs, but he played the game marvelously. I'm sure he hurt a lot of people deeply and gave them no credit, but then he sang their songs so well that they might not have gotten out there if he didn't. Think about it; there is this guy who wrote that song and he's listening to it on the radio and his name's not even on it. Talk about hell on earth. It's like carving a monolith of your girlfriend that turns into the Eiffel Tower or the Statue of Liberty and nobody knows you did it.

Bob Dylan. The way people perceive him is twisted. He's truly a sage and a bard, but I think we all are, except when we start to believe it, we lose that gift of the energy therein.

John Lennon. He was the yin for McCartney's yang.

129

BANDS I WISH I'D BEEN IN
The Everly Brothers
Eric Burdon and the original Animals
The Pretty Things
Bill Monroe and the Bluegrass Boys

FAMOUS PHOTOGRAPHS I WISH I HAD BEEN IN
The Hindenburg in flames

The astronauts planting the flag on the moon

A BED I'D LIKE TO HAVE BEEN IN
Napoleon's with the print of bees all over it—and
experienced what he experienced in it

SOMEONE'S SHOES I WOULDN'T MIND BEING IN
The moon boots worn by Wally Schirra

TRAILS I WISH I HAD BEEN ON
Certainly not Donner's Pass, where they all got
cannibalized.
I'd like to have been Montezuma's left-hand man and
blown Cortez away with a flame-thrower so his skull and
eyeballs cracked and sizzled.

A COUPLE OF THINGS THAT TICK ME OFF
Teachers who don't know how to teach

The fact that you need a license to drive a car, yet
anybody can be a parent

TEACHERS I WISH I HAD AT SCHOOL
Leo Buscaglia, on love. People think love is a fuck flick.

Mother Teresa on the virtues of giving it away. You can't
get it back unless you give it away.

Joseph Campbell on the power of myth

SOMEONE I WOULDN'T MIND SITTING NEXT TO ON A PLANE
The lieutenant from Andrews Air Force Base who told me
he was part of the troop that was driven in a bus with
the windows blacked out so they didn't know where
they were going, and when they reached their destination
they found a crashed saucer and dead aliens

A QUESTION I OFTEN ASK MYSELF
If men bled, would tampons be free?

IF I WERE A LADY
I'd wear lace like Stevie Nicks (although she's a little too
chunky nowadays),
dress like Joan Collins,
have Madonna's free spirit,
Cher's ass (which is forever),
and have a face like the model who was in *Weird Science*
and *Lady in Red*—Kelly LeBrock.

POETS WHO INSPIRE ME MOST
Lennon and McCartney
Rudyard Kipling
Brian Wilson

A COUPLE OF MINOR MASTERPIECES
"Think About It," the Yardbirds
"All for the Love of a Girl," Johnny Horton

THE FIRST EXPENSIVE THING I BOUGHT WITH MY FIRST BIG PAYCHECK
A big bag of pistachio nuts. Until we got our first advance
from CBS, we all lived in an apartment together and I
spent my money on Boone's Farm and blue crystal meth,
which I kept in the refrigerator.

A BOX OF CEREAL I'D LIKE TO BE ON
Kellogg's Frosted Flakes

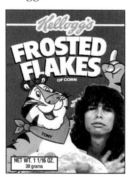

AN INTERSECTION I'D LIKE TO DIRECT TRAFFIC AT
The one under the L'Arc de Triomphe in Paris. You can
spend years in there and not get out. It's the worst
cloverleaf in the world. No insurance company will insure
you if you're in an accident there.

MAGAZINES I SUBSCRIBE TO
Berkeley Wellness Letter
Cherry Pop Tart Comix

THINGS I KEEP NEXT TO MY BED
My affirmations book
My shotgun from my childhood
An eight-inch switchblade

THREE THINGS ON MY WISH LIST
Follow Joe Perry's lead guitar with a kazoo

Be the house band on the shuttle to the moon

Spend the night with two bisexual porn stars who haven't
been fucked by John Holmes

IN MY HEART OF HEARTS
I'm nothing more than a channel. Everything I ever heard, I
just took in. Everybody hears stuff differently, so
consequently I heard it my way. My father's a classical
pianist; I grew up under the piano. I learned the
language of music—the emotions of life—through my
father. Listen to Debussy's "Claire de Lune." There's so
much emotion; I give my daughter baths to that.

NEAREST FARAWAY PLACE
The attic—where I can go and pretend,
sit all alone, meditate,
go back to any place I ever was when I was a kid. I can
pretend I was in Moohahooka Island, flying freely over the
ocean, two inches above the surface, watching porpoises
play. I can sit on a rock in
the middle of a stream and smell the water. That's my attic.
I just got to wipe the cobwebs off my hair.

Aretha Franklin

SOME EARLY INFLUENCES
The Clara Ward Singers
James Cleveland
Ruth Brown
Dinah Washington
"Why Do Fools Fall in Love?" Frankie Lymon and
the Teenagers
"My Little Suede Shoes," Charlie Parker
"Tweedlee Dee," LaVern Baker

SOME PEOPLE I'D LIKE TO SING A DUET WITH
Stevie Wonder
Smokey Robinson
Michael McDonald

THREE THINGS THAT GET ME UP IN THE MORNING
"The Guiding Light"
"The Bold and the Beautiful"
"The Young and the Restless"

SOME MOVIES I LIKE FALLING ASLEEP TO
Dr. Zhivago
An Affair to Remember, with Rock Hudson
and Deborah Kerr
Lady Sings the Blues

A COUPLE OF HOUSEHOLD HINTS
Remove gum stuck in your carpet with an ice cube
Clorox whitens stains in the sink.

MY IDEA OF A SEXY SINGER
Marvin Gaye

MY FAVORITE PISTON
Joe Dumars

BOOKS ON MY BEST-SELLER LIST
Conversations with Bette Davis
Dream Girl
Jim Brown
Winning Against the Odds, by John H. Johnson

A WORD NOT IN MY VOCABULARY
The blues

SOME MAGAZINES I SUBSCRIBE TO
Ebony
Jet
Women's Wear Daily
Architectural Digest

A FEW OF MY FAVORITE DESIGNERS
Valentino
Bill Blass
Caroline Rhoem
Issey Miyake
Thierry Mugler
Donna Karan

MY FAVORITE ARCHITECTURE
Contemporary
French chateaus
French regency
Some Frank Lloyd Wright

FIRST EXTRAVAGENT THING I BOUGHT
White roller skates with toe stops, big fluffy balls on the shoe laces, and Fomac and Ray Besto wheels. I bought them when I was in a little skate shop in Detroit called the Arcadia, with the money my dad had given me after we had performed at a church service.

MOST VALUED POSSESSIONS
Let's just say I'm a romantic; that'll cover everything.

John Taylor

THE HISTORY OF MUSIC

As far as I'm concerned, it doesn't exist before the Beatles.
From that moment on, pop became packaged, with
carefully designed sleeves and album cover photographs.
In pop music, the photograph is important. By
the time Duran Duran made records, videos were even
more important.

MY IDEA OF A SOUL SINGER

Bryan Ferry solo music. The first time I listened to original
rock 'n' roll was when we made *Notorious*. I wasn't
even aware of Black music until Chic. Chic wasn't disco.
They were the hippest rock 'n' roll band. I lost all my
friends over them. They were as powerful as the Sex
Pistols. They loved English pop music. Chic was the name
that came closest to Roxy Music. Roxy Music was
important to post-'70s English bands because of their
album covers. They named the model on the cover. They
wore false leopard skin and had greasy hair. They were a
complete parody of everything, the ultimate
art-school band.

THE EVENT IN HISTORY DURAN DURAN WOULD LIKE TO HAVE WITNESSED

Woodstock—even more than the parting of the Red Sea or
the Crucifixion

WHAT PISSES ME OFF

When I go into Charivari's and pick out something and the
salesman tells me Nick's already beat me to it.
(But it pisses me off more when the salesman *doesn't*
tell me.)

Nick Rhodes

A BAND THAT MADE A DIFFERENCE

The Velvet Undergound. They were incredibly original. They looked really great in wraparound shades and black clothes when everybody else wore horrible paisley shirts and a smile. The Velvet Underground also sang fantastic songs like "All Tomorrow's Parties" and "Venus in Furs," even though they couldn't play their instruments that well. I always liked bands with an image.

TWO BIGGEST MUSICAL INFLUENCES

Crazy Eddie
Jacoby and Meyers' law firm TV commercials

THE CONCEPT OF DURAN DURAN

It started out as a dreamscape, an unformidable animal, something that was modern and innovative. I guess innovators get a lot of flak in the beginning. We never wanted to be a rock 'n' roll band. We wanted to be a surreal pop group. At first we had a real cult audience. Then suddenly came the mass exposure, and exposure has to do with light, and the light blinded a lot of people. Now the lens has just closed up a little bit and people can get the full picture. It's starting to click.

HOW DURAN DURAN STARTED

John and I have always been spiritually closest because we grew up together —in Hollywood, Birmingham, which is a lot cooler to come from than Hollywood, California. (We met drummer Roger Taylor in Birmingham.) We put an ad in *Melody Maker* saying we were looking for a guitar player who was a cross between Mick Ronson, Dave Gilmore (from Pink Floyd), and Carlos Alomar—someone who could play atmospheric stuff like Gilmore, had the power of Mick Ronson, and was

funky like Alomar. That's how we got Andy Taylor. Simon Le Bon was studying drama at the University at Birmingham when we got him through a bar maid at the Rum Runner. She was his ex-girlfriend. There were two hip clubs in England at the time the punk scene was dying down, the Runner in Birmingham, and the Blitz in London. Punk was made up of Roxy Music, David Bowie, Sparks, and Cockney Rebel fans; it wasn't so much a heavy duty street scene, conceptual and as far away from Yes as we could possibly get, more like the glam rock bands of the '70s, like Roxy Music and T-Rex.

When we first met Simon, he was a drama queen. I couldn't believe it. He was like a camp actor. He was like something out of British '60s films. He could quote things from almost any Velvet Underground song. He arrived at the audition with his book, which was this scrawny looking thing with the most perverse

lyrics in it. People just do not give him credit for his lyrics, maybe because some of them are so pretentious. But all I ever wanted Duran Duran to be, more than anything else, was a surreal pop group.

More than anything else, Simon had a good attitude. He really wanted to do the music we were making. On top of that, he did look a little bit strange. He had this bleached orangy kind of hair and these black shiny boots. Before I heard him sing a note, I told everybody he was in the group. Our management tried to persuade us for months to get another singer because he couldn't sing properly. He was singing out of tune at our concerts but John and I were saying it didn't matter if he sings out of tune. We were looking for a singer who was a cross between Lou Reed, Iggy Pop, and David Bowie, mashed into one. We didn't think Simon was exactly all that, but he was original. He didn't

sound like anybody else. He wasn't a crooner
like Bryan Ferry, but he had something special. We had

already been through ten singers before Simon, and
after that, Simon was a real breath of fresh air. At least he
got four out of five notes on pitch.

ONE SONG I WISH SIMON HAD NEVER WRITTEN
"My Own Way"

A WOMAN I'D LIKE TO BE
Joan Crawford, just because she wore great shoulder pads.

SOMEBODY DURAN DURAN WOULD RATHER BE
Roger Vadim—for the amount of time he was in bed with
all those great women: Brigitte Bardot, Catherine Deneuve,
and Jane Fonda

THE FRUIT I'D LIKE TO BE
Some people like to go off and live in the country and hike
up mountains every day. Some people like to stay
in a small town and live from nine to five. Others aspire to
more erratic patterns, maybe something more exciting,
maybe something that is more of a gamble, maybe
something that can be totally crushing. I think everybody
has a streak in them that's only present in them and not in
anybody else. I like to wear nice suits. You can
say that Bruce Springsteen likes to wear blue jeans and a
T-shirt. I wouldn't feel comfortable in blue jeans
and a T-shirt. I'm sure Bruce wouldn't feel comfortable in
one of my suits, but what I wear doesn't make a difference
about how I see things or how I write music. I
think fashion is a very important part of youth culture. It
always has been. It's very closely related to music.

Every band who has made it big had an image, whether
it be the Beatles in their black suits, the
Rolling Stones with their slightly more tough look, Pink
Floyd with their psychedelic suits, or us with
the frilly shirts when we came out. It's all something that
should never be taken too seriously, but at the same time
it's important to come across with some kind
of unified, identifiable front. The other thing is, perhaps I
view fashion in a different sense than most people in that
fashion has to do with attitude, fashion has
to do with being modern. I don't just think about clothes, I

think about furniture, light fittings, door handles,
magazines, window displays, cars, fruit. I sometimes sit
and muse to myself, God, the person who
designed fruit must have been cool, but the person in the
vegetable department wasn't quite so together.
I mean potatoes and carrots are real drab, but when you
look at pineapples, wow!

THE PURVEYORS OF GREAT TASTE
Early on I thought it was great to get our picture in a
magazine. Andy Warhol said that he never read his press,
but he always weighed it, and if it was heavy,
then he knew everything was O.K. I kind of went along
with that regime for a while. I thought as long
as people were talking it was good, but more recently I
realized that when I wanted to talk seriously
about some aspect of Duran Duran or life in general,
people already had so many preconceived ideas about me
and the band, and I found that pretty depressing.
The idea of all these people out there thinking they know
me a little bit because they read about me in
the newspaper, where in fact they probably know less
about me than the people who don't know me at all,
bothers me. In the beginning it never mattered who liked
Duran Duran. What was important was the fact
that somebody liked us. We always made music primarily
for ourselves. Most groups do. I don't know who our
audience is. I guess the only time you get to
find out is when you play live gigs and see who turns up.
All I'd say to the cynics who say we're a group
for little girls is, I think little girls are great. They make a
lot of noise, they're excited, and they're hip because they're
the first ones to catch on. They were certainly the
first ones to catch on to the Beatles, the Rolling Stones, the
Doors, David Bowie, and any other people who
basically became rock legends.

Simon Le Bon

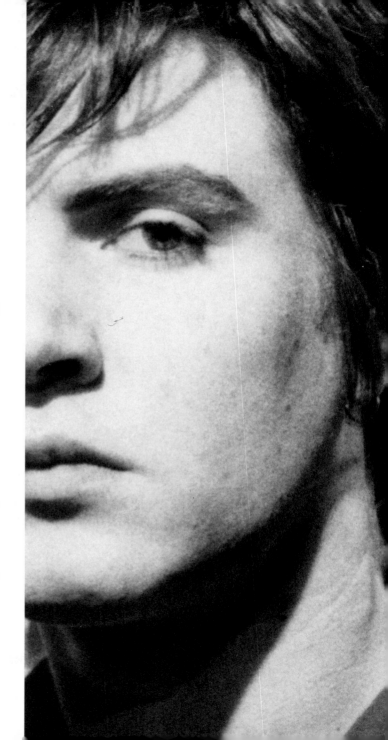

MY LIFE SO FAR
Everything has been sudden. Nothing has been gradual.
Suddenly I'm doing this. Suddenly I'm doing that. I was
in university one week and in a pop group the next.
Success came quick. It wasn't a struggle, but there was a
personal struggle: trying to get into a band and being
accepted by the other members. That took a year, not until
after our first album; then I felt accepted.

THE DURAN DURAN MEMBER WHO GOT THE MOST GIRLS
John, usually. Sometimes we'd go to a party or a club and
feel like a dog in a car park when all the cars
were leaving, trying to make our mind up and ending
up with nothing.

HOW I MET JASMINE
On a blind date, except it wasn't a totally blind date
because I had already seen a photo of her in a
photographer's portfolio. I took her to the premiere of
Indiana Jones and the Temple of Doom. We liked
each other immediately after finishing a bottle of scotch. A
month after we were married, I was at a hotel in
Australia, sitting by the pool, next to a girl, and a
photographer, who was on the roof of a building a mile
away, took a picture and sent it back to England.
A headline in a newspaper said, "Simon Le Bon Cheats on
His Wife Thirty Days After Their Wedding." I
haven't forgiven that paper since.

HOW TO LET A GIRL DOWN EASY
Just don't take her to a restaurant. That way, she won't
throw food at you. Take her to a nightclub instead, and
point her in the direction of someone new.

MY FAVORITE CLUBS

The Hell Fire Club and any of the Roman baths, which were like clubs where people watched people swim instead of dance. I would skip the medieval clubs, because there weren't any: People back then were too afraid to go out, so they invited everybody to their castle. But I don't think I would have been invited. It's surprising that clubs today don't have a moat and drawbridge outside the front door to keep people out and in.

A PHOTOGRAPH DURAN DURAN WISHES THEY WERE IN

Raising the flag at Iwo Jima, except we don't look good in uniforms. We would have to be shot from chin up.

SIX INFLUENTIAL RECORDS
"Can I Get a Witness," Public Enemy
"I Ain't No Joke," Erik B. and Rakim
"Cigarettes and Coffee," Otis Redding
"Your Precious Love," Marvin Gaye and Tammi Terrell
"Rainbow," Gene Chandler
"Papa Don't Take No Mess," James Brown

THREE FAVORITE FRED WILLIAMSON MOVIES
Black Caesar
Hell Up in Harlem
Three the Hard Way

FAVORITE POETS
Smokey Robinson
Grand Master Caz

FIRST EXPENSIVE THING I BOUGHT
A fat gold rope chain

A COUPLE OF PEOPLE ON MY BEST-DRESSED LIST
Dr. Jekyll
Mr. Hyde

DEFINITION OF DEF
A red Mercedes convertible, with a big fat Ferarri kit,
hammer rims, and lights going across the front grill.

FAVORITE BARBER
Denny Mo up in Harlem

A CLUB I BELONG TO
The Players' Ball

TIPS FOR GIRLS WHO WANT ME TO LIKE THEM
Don't speak to me with all that B-boy-B-girl stuff.
Don't be dingy.

IF I WERE A WOMAN
I'd like to be Janet Jackson.

THREE THINGS THAT GET THE JOB DONE
Cash
Credit cards
My tongue

SOMETHING I CAN'T DO BUT WISH I COULD
Sing

John Cale

WHERE I'M FROM

Garmant, Wales—a small community of terrace housing squashed together inside a small valley. On one side was one little coal mine and on the other were the sheep farmers. Most of the people were miners. My father was a coal miner. My mother was a teacher.

WHAT I LISTENED TO

Radio Luxembourg—I would listen to every piece of classical music and then every Friday night at 7:00, bingo, there would be Alan Freed, "for your listening pleasure," with all the top ten hits from America. The teddy boys came from that program and I was the local teddy boy.

WHAT I DIDN'T LISTEN TO

My mother—she taught me piano until I went to grammar school. Then she thought I should spend more time studying law or medicine, so I wouldn't end up in the coal mines like my father. The minute that happened, the more time I spent playing piano. The harder my mother pushed me in the direction of money, the harder I pushed toward music.

MY FIRST INSTRUMENT

The viola—there was an allocation of instruments at school, but when it came my turn to pick one, there weren't any violins left. There weren't many people who played viola and there weren't many people who played it well, and if you did play it well, you were a big fish in a small pond. There is no way to play rock 'n' roll on a viola.

HOW I GOT TO AMERICA

I studied composition at London University's Goldsmith's College, worked on a musicological dissertation and listened to avant-garde and electronic music. I was unaware that the Rolling Stones were playing in a club down the block. Instead I paid attention to who was playing which instrument in which orchestra. The biggest thing about listening to an orchestra was figuring out which section was the weakest link. Slowly you got to know the names of personnel and that knowledge became impressive. Around the time I met Aaron Copland in London 1963—about getting a scholarship at Tanglewood—I was paying a lot of attention to who was playing what on the recordings of John Cage, David Tudor and Robert Kraft. I had written John Cage to see if we could work together when I was at Tanglewood and he said to call. So basically what I was saying to Copland was if I got the scholarship or not, I'm going to America.

WHAT AARON COPLAND SAID

"I can't promise you any performances of your work, because they seem to be very violent." Copland was not impressed with my work but by how much I knew about all these musicians. He seemed to be very impressed that I got in touch with Cage. He saw me as someone trying to do something. I was 21.

WHY CAGE

Unlike most conductors who tell musicians how to play a piece, Cage gave his musicians the freedom to play however they wanted. But Cage had already passed the baton on to LaMonte Young, saying he was the most interesting composer in America. After the summer in Tanglewood I moved to the Lower East Side and worked with Young for almost a year, until I got a better job with the Velvet Underground.

HOW I MET LOU REED

I had been at some guy's apartment and someone comes up to me and says, "You look very commercial, I'd like you to come over to the record company." I went up to Pickwick and there was Lou making coffee. Lou worked as a song writer. He had made a single called "The Ostrich" and needed a backup band to go out and promote it, which we —me, Lou, Tony Conrad who was also working with LaMonte and Cage, and Walter De Maria—did, as the Primitives. In the meantime Lou was pointing out all the songs he had done that Pickwick wouldn't allow him to record, like "Heroin." So I said, let's do it ourselves. We went up to 125 Street in Harlem, sat on the sidewalk outside a blues club called the Baby Grand—Lou with his guitar, me with my viola—and made a nice splash of money until the cops came and told us to move along. We spent a year where Lou came in every Friday from wherever he lived on Long Island and we'd rehearse until we got some pretty interesting arrangements. The product was the banana album (*The Velvet Underground & Nico*).

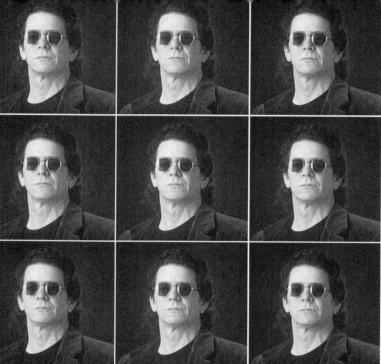

there, because these were people who were experts at them and I wasn't. Andy was the expert. Lou was completely spooked by him; he didn't understand what made this man tick. Lou's was an endless search to find the button. But I got so much enjoyment out of bouncing ideas back and forth with Andy that for me it was great, whatever it was. There was a certain intellectual quirk, however, that put me off. The repetition that I found in Andy's work I had been aware of from being with LaMonte; I thought Andy came late in the day to repetition, but I since learned that was not true. He was probably the closest collaborator that anybody would want to have. For all the ideas that Lou and I came up with, as insubordinate as they were to anything that was artistically viable at the time, he was the guy supporting it and telling us not to forget about it. He was definitely a co-conspirator in all of it. We'd spend the day at the Factory and wind up at the Gingerman every night to watch the fight between Edie Sedgwick and Andy.

HOW LOU AND I GOT ON

Lou and I had one of these terrible rapports where you think the other guy is thinking what you're thinking, but he's not. He couldn't figure me out, and I couldn't figure him out. The only thing we had in common were drugs and this obsession with risk taking. That was the raison d'etre for the Velvet Underground. We both had tremendous drive and determination and we both hit out at anything that came our way. Flower Power? Get out of here. Give people hard drugs. Give them the drugs they want. Acid? Fuck off. Heroin. Amphetamine. It wasn't so much the flavor of the drug; it was the mentality involved that we really resented. The mentality of the West Coast was so vapid and directionless. We thought doing evil was better than doing nothing.

WHAT WE ENDED UP DOING

We'd get up at two in the afternoon and go up to Andy Warhol's Factory. I went with a purpose: to work. I wasn't involved in playing the games they played up

WHY I WAS KICKED OUT OF THE VELVET UNDERGROUND

We were getting ready to go to Cleveland in 1969 and Lou
got Mo [Maureen] and Sterling together and said, "If Cale
goes to Cleveland I don't go." That was it. We
got to the end of our tether. Obviously there was a lot of
competition, although when Lou and I fought,
it was over ideas and how to resolve them. By the time we
made *White Light/White Heat*, we were a road band and it
slowly eroded our confidence, our ego, our
persona, so things went from bad to worse. The music got
to be entirely secondary; there was too much
social antics and acrimony going on. I figured I could be a
producer. I wanted to write songs. I needed to go
out and prove to myself that I was my own person again.
Also, Lou brought a manager in who was a
snake of the first order and fed the insidiousness of the
situation and was instrumental in splitting us. He favored
Lou. He said he writes the songs, he's the guy.
So I had to go out and get another job.

THE JOB I GOT

Producing Iggy and the Stooges first album—Iggy's a very
normal, well-adjusted fellow who has this magical ability
to change his persona. He's like a chameleon.

Nico—In 1971, when she was doing *Marble Index*, she was
working in a completely European tradition that
was startling in its difference and focus from anything
other female singers were doing around that time. Almost
enough to start her own culture. She studied
with Elia Kazan, and he told her that whatever she did, do
it in your own time, and she took that advice,
boy, and built a whole lifestyle around it. Her sense of
timing was extraordinary. Everything about her style was
very paced. You'd have to adjust your body clock
to a totally different scale to be around her. Her life wasn't
something you wanted to observe all the time; it
was better to walk in and out of, like a play. She was the
original Robert Wilson play;
Jonathan Richman and the Modern Lovers—Jonathan had
this tape with "Hospital" and all these other
songs that were so quirky and naive. Warner Brothers
went to great lengths to promote them, they
flew in managers from all over but Jonathan just became
contrary; success was probably not what he wanted.

SOMETHING I MISSED

Performing. It was obvious to me after doing my *Paris 1919*
and *Academy* that I couldn't just do albums in a vacuum.
You got to go out and promote them. You got to
go and do the stuff that Lou had undertaken years ago, to
put your ass on the line and perform. Making *Fear* and
Slow Dazzle was a chance to do it. I tried to recreate the
Velvet Underground, but I wasn't successful.

HOW LOU AND I GOT BACK TOGETHER

We were at the party following Andy's memorial service.
It was the first time we had spoken to each other
since the Velvet Underground—we bumped into each
other a lot of times before but he wasn't interested
in communicating, probably because I was still drinking.
First Julian Schnabel came up to me and bulldozed
the idea through. He said, "Look, you got to
do something for Andy." I replied it would be a bit tough
to do anything now. "No, no, let's you and me
get together and write something." Then he said, "Let's get
Lou over here." I thought, what the hell is
Julian doing? Does he always do this for people? The last
time I saw him, he was a busboy at the Lower
Manhattan Ocean Club and now that he's got these
paintings with the plates smashed all over them, he's got a
whole new view of life. A few days later, Lou
and I agreed to do a collaboration. In ten days we wrote
fourteen songs for *'Drella*. It was one way of dealing
with the past. There were other things I wanted to do, that
were more difficult than *'Drella*, Lou and I
could do a lot. We can now get on with something more
ambitious.

DESIGNING JOHN
Betsey Johnson:
I met John in Max's when the Velvet Underground wanted
me to do their clothes. I was so excited, because
I thought they would want to rock out, but Lou wanted
basically a Levi's jacket and jeans in grey suede, and I don't
like designing like that so much. Sterling and Maureen
liked velvet, so I did a lot of studded velvet. But John
wanted me to make costumes where his hands would go
on fire. He'd wear masks all the time and I thought, this is
my kind of guy. I ended up making him tight black
Edwardian suits made of canvas, with ruffles and bows.

Before John and I got married, we lived together at
the Chelsea Hotel, then on a loft on LaGuardia
Place where Nico lived under our kitchen sink. When we
decided to get married, all the Velvets were
against it, probably because John was the first to have
a girl come into the group. I think Lou saw it as a
threat; John and Lou always had a star problem. I'm sure
that Lou didn't personally dislike me, but he thought I
could cut a good pair of pants. We were going to have this
funky wedding at City Hall. *Ladies Home Journal* found out
about it and were going to throw this big bash afterwards,
so they could photograph the freaky rock 'n' roll scene.
About a week before the wedding, John went to the
hospital for a blood test because he was turning brought
yellow. Sure enough, John had hepatitis and stayed in the
hospital for four months. *Ladies Home Journal* wanted
me to go ahead with the wedding without John; they said
they'd just take a picture of him and strip it in later.

WHAT GOES ON

Things will take care of themselves. That's because I was brought up rich. My old man was an accountant; he wanted me to take over the company.
I had street punk sense with money to pour down the drain. I'm used to people taking care of me, but in my particular case, I'm not a spoiled rich kid. I just did enough groovy things so people tolerated me. Even when I was poor I was this way and people took care of me.
I mean, I haven't even got past eight years old in most ways. Andy: If you're not looking for it, it'll show up. Me: Things will take care of themselves. It's a good introduction to how things work.

WHAT I DID INSTEAD OF TAKING OVER THE COMPANY

Became a staff writer at Pickwick International in late '64, early '65, part of a group of four who put out ninety-nine-cent budget albums you'd see in Woolworth's or supermarkets. Some were all-surfing records with made-up names and we would write and perform them—very quickly. All that while I was writing my other stuff, which was perfromed by the Velvet Underground, which they didn't want to hear about at Pickwick.

MY EARLY IDOLS

Gerry Goffin and Carole King

FOR THE RECORD

The first record, *The Velvet Underground & Nico*, was cut basically in three hours. We just wanted to make a record. We didn't know good equipment. It wasn't even a matter in those days whether it was good equipment, it was just did it work? In those days, engineers would walk out on us anyway: "I didn't become an engineer so I could listen to you guys jerk off."
I saw what the Velvets sold. Zero. The "Heroin" song on the Mercury album is fabulous. The original is fabulous.
But *Rock & Roll Animal*, what a degrading thing. And I actually went through with it just to get popular so I could get the Velvets things out. That's why I made *Sally Can't Dance*. Can you imagine putting out *Sally Can't Dance* with your name on it? Dyeing my hair and all that shit. That's what they wanted and that's what they got. When *Sally Can't Dance* went into the top ten without even a single, I said to myself, what a piece of shit. That has to be one of the lowest albums, except for

Rock & Roll Animal. Like none of the pictures of me over those years even vaguely looked like me.

I don't like *Lou Reed Live* or *Transformer*. I don't like "Walk on the Wild Side" because I know how it should be done. The song was a big hit because it was banned from all the radio stations. But it did do what it was supposed to do. Like I said, I wanted to get popular so I got the biggest shlocks around and I turned out really big shlock, because my shit's better than most people's diamonds. But it's really boring to be the best show in town.

Berlin nearly killed us. When [producer] Bobby Ezrin gave me the master he said, "Don't even listen to it, just put it in a drawer," and he went back to Canada and flipped out. So they use that album as an example of how bad I got. I know I stay away from the album as much as I can.

Some people told me *Metal Machine* would ruin my career. They said it was a ripoff. They said it was immoral to take money for that. I guess I'm immoral then. I really love *Metal Machine*. It cleans me out. I was thinking about *Metal Machine* for years. I just waited until I was powerful enough to put it out. They were supposed to put out a disclaimer: *Listen to it first: no vocals. Best cut: none. Sounds like: static on the car radio.*

MY FAVORITE LOU REED SONG

Nico doing "I'll Be Your Mirror"

A MAGAZINE THAT REJECTED MY POETRY

The New Yorker, when I wanted to be a *New Yorker* poet. I'd get a letter from a secretary or someone who felt sorry for me and say I had potential and to keep up the good work but they had all the poetry they needed for the next fifteen years.
I used to get *Writer's Market* which told you all the books that take poetry, like *The Kenyon Review, The Hudson Review, The Paris Review,* but later it dawned on me, who wants to be published in these magazines anyway? I was in *The Harvard Advocate,* though. And some of my songs end up in magazines as poems.

COLORS I IDENTIFY WITH MOST

Black and white, although gold has gotten interesting. Black and white has so many possibilities. You can have a

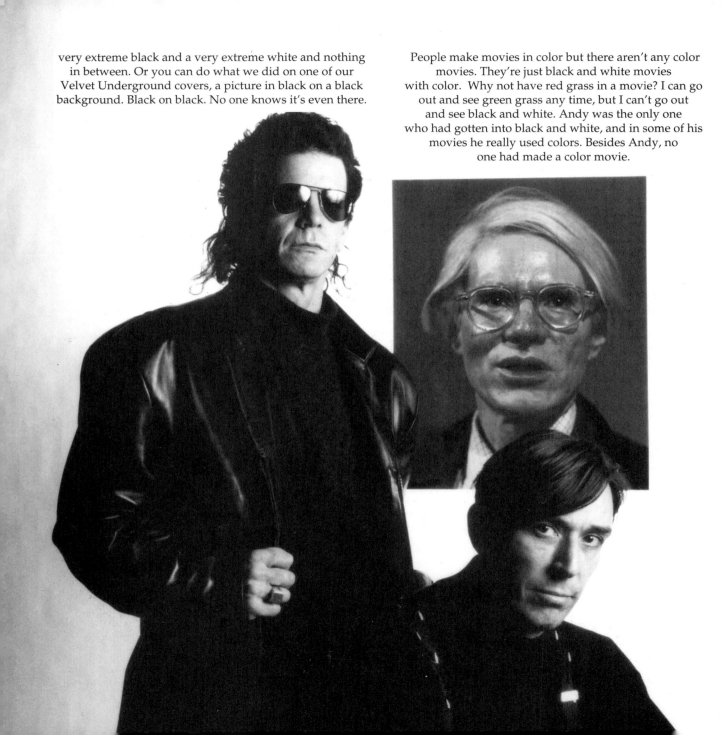

very extreme black and a very extreme white and nothing in between. Or you can do what we did on one of our Velvet Underground covers, a picture in black on a black background. Black on black. No one knows it's even there.

People make movies in color but there aren't any color movies. They're just black and white movies with color. Why not have red grass in a movie? I can go out and see green grass any time, but I can't go out and see black and white. Andy was the only one who had gotten into black and white, and in some of his movies he really used colors. Besides Andy, no one had made a color movie.

HOW I MET ANDY WARHOL

The Velvet Underground was playing at the Cafe Bizarre, a
tourist trap in Greenwich Village, and some mutual
friends brought him down the night we got fired. The club
manager said, "You guys play one more song like
that and that's it ." So we did ["The Black Angel's Death
Song"] and she fired us.

A THING OF BEAUTY

A 1940 Harley Davidson Low Glide. You can hang
the engine on the wall, its so beautiful, but it's a lot better
if you put a gas tank on top of it, a seat, and go riding.

THE DEFINITION OF MACHO

A two-bit word used to describe an A-bomb. What's
macho? Is Einstein macho? What's macho? Somebody
swinging? Somebody using karate? How about a sound
gun? How about using lasers? Is macho a good fuck? You
can just put it in, come and leave. It becomes very
predictable and can' t be very interesting. It's like going to
bed with someone and saying "I'm bored" and it's only
been five minutes. Imagine getting married and finding out
a year later you must have been really stupid. And even
stupider if you don't get your ass out of there.
Complaining isn't very macho. Not making it isn't macho.
Not making an effort to get across to other people is not
very macho. Just having street smarts is not very macho.
Being intellectual and having street smarts is a little better.
But there should be a point past there. What's macho?
Times Square? Is Neil Young macho? He's envious of the
Southern thing, that's his problem. Is fucking that
facinating after awhile? Are you sure? Are you positive?
Doesn't it get a little tiring and monotonous after
awhile? What about bad breath in the morning? What
about being afraid to be alone? Aren't you tired
of yourself? Why don't you hang yourself out to dry? I
was tired of me really early. I bring me out periodically,
but after awhile, I run out of patience.

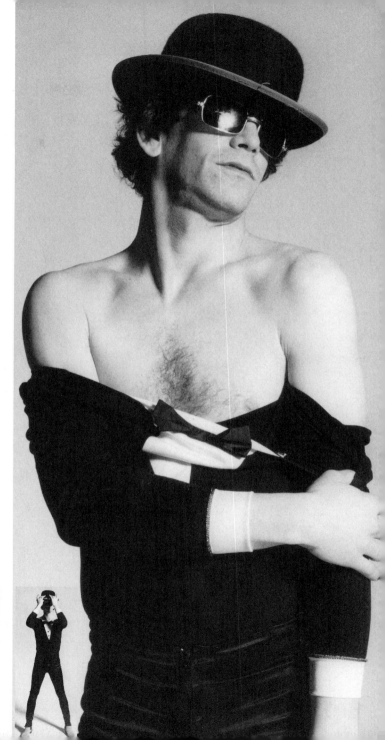

Chrissie Hynde

A TURNING POINT IN MY LIFE

One afternoon when I was fourteen, my girlfriends and I went to see Mitch Ryder and the Detroit Wheels at Chippewa Lake Park Appreciation Day. There was a fight up on stage and I was so knocked out with it that I stayed on to see the show in the evening. Then they had a fight up on stage again and I realized I had been duped. But I liked the guitar player. He played good, and naturally if you played good you looked good. He looked like he was plugged in.

ROCK STARS I'D LIKE TO HAVE BEEN

Brian Jones—Like every teenager in the 1960s. I was more inclined to be Brian Jones than to want to sleep with him. I wasn't thinking about all that when I was fourteen. I was thinking about how cool it was to wear white trousers and a striped shirt, have a Vox teardrop guitar, and be able to play harmonica in a really rocking band.

The Beatles—My ultimate favorites. The Rolling Stones were gutsy and rock 'n' roll, but the Beatles were real poetry with great harmonies and melodies. There was something about the Beatles that wasn't of this world.

The Kinks—People fail to recognize how much the Beatles and the Stones were influenced by the Kinks. All you have to do is listen to something like "Autumn Almanac" and you'll hear it all, especially in some of Dave Davies' chops. He made that great quote: "It wasn't called heavy metal when I invented it."

Bob Dylan—I learned guitar by looking at the Bob Dylan song books.

Jimi Hendrix—I thought he was very happening and still do, especially when I look at who's out there now.

The Velvet Underground—They were a dark band who made a noise that appealed to me.

James Brown—There should be a statue of him in every park in America. He had the greatest influence of anyone in contemporary music.

MY ALL TIME-HERO
Iggy Pop—although I came in after the fact. I didn't really get into Iggy until the *Raw Power* album.

SOMEONE I WOULD HAVE TRADED BODIES WITH
Jeff Beck. Just to get my hands on a guitar like he did.

PEOPLE I WOULDN'T MIND SMELLING, BEING NEAR, TOUCHING
Patrick Macnee—He played Steed on "The Avengers." Bo Bo Bolinski—"believe me, folks, I'm not a big deal"—in R. Crumb comic books.

SOMEONE I CAN'T IMAGINE BEING
Myself as people see me. When I see myself in a video or listen to my records, that's not me.

HOW I GOT MY BANGS
I saw a picture of Jane Asher in *16 Magazine* when I was fourteen. She was an actress and Paul McCartney's big flame for years, before he met Linda. Jane Ascher had ginger hair, which I thought was very cool. That was kind of like a greaser thing; they always had their hair dyed red or black.

THE ONLY REAL WOMAN FOR ME
Jean Shrimpton. She was the only model for me. I said that to David Bailey, who's been with some of the most beautiful women in the world, and he agreed.

AN EARLY PREMONITION

When I was twelve, my teacher told everyone in class to write down their favorite word on a piece of paper and put it face down on the desk. Then she told us to write a poem about the word. My word was *England*. The poem was almost a complete prediction of everything I did in the next twenty years.

MY FIRST INSTRUMENT

A ukulele

MY FIRST GIG

When I was sixteen I did a little stint with Mark Mothersbaugh, who later became Devo.

MY FIRST GUITAR

A Melody Maker. My folks bought it for my twenty-first birthday. It was advertised in the paper for sixty dollars. I traded it shortly thereafter at a music store for a hollow-body Ovation guitar. Then I sold the Ovation and split for England and France. Meanwhile my girlfriend went to the music store and bought the Melody Maker. In 1975, when I went back to Cleveland to join a band, I borrowed the Melody Maker off of her. One night it got stolen out of the trunk of a car, so Duane, the bass player in the band, brought another Melody Maker for me to use but it needed new strings. So we went to some guitar store and I saw some guy walk by with my Melody Maker; I could tell the machine heads had just been changed. I could have gotten it back, but I would have had to press charges against the kid who stole it.

WHY I WENT TO ENGLAND

Because I was influenced by a picture of Iggy Pop that was in *New Musical Express* which I framed and hung on my wall. I went there in 1973 because I thought everyone in England was interested in the kind of music I dug.

WHAT I BROUGHT ALONG WITH ME

One suitcase and three albums: *White Light/White Heat*, *Raw Power*, and *Fun House*. I brought the records along because I thought I might need a fix somewhere along the line. About three months after I got there I lent the records to some guy and he left the country.

BANDS I COULD HAVE BEEN IN

Back in Cleveland I got a letter from Malcolm McLaren saying he was forming a band called the Love Boys and he wanted me fronting the band as a boy. He even offered to send me a ticket, but I declined, because I was in a band called Jack Rabbit at the time.

When I ended up back in England in 1976, I met this guy Bernie Rose, who was a sort of competitor of Malcolm McClaren's. Bernie had the idea of calling a band School Girls' Underpants. I didn't want to have anything to do with that.

Malcolm was going to have another band with two singers—a real fair guy and a real dark guy—a drummer, a bass player, and me on guitar. It was going to be called the Masters of the Backside. As soon as we worked out quite a few songs, the singer, the bass player—who later changed his name to Captain Sensible—and the drummer—who changed his name to Rat Scabies—went off and got together a band called The Damned.

The Johnny Mopeds—I used to work a lot with them. I got with just about every band in town, but everyone always went off to do something else and I got left behind. I didn't fit in, maybe because I was American and I was a couple years older and had been around a lot more and they were London kids who were part of the punk explosion.

WHERE THE NAME PRETENDERS CAME FROM

David Hill called up and said they were pressing our record ["Precious"] and we needed a name immediately. The night before I had been talking to this greaser chick I knew about this London Hell's Angel we knew and how he'd go into his room and bolt the door shut so none of the brothers could come in and he'd put on the record "The Great Pretender." "The Great Pretender" was his alter ego. So I told David to call it the Pretenders.

SOMETHING I DID BEFORE I WAS A MUSICIAN

Painted—but not commercial painting. I didn't want to use any talent or skill I had for anything other than being creative. I would rather have been a waitress and paint on weekends. But I didn't want to be a waitress, either.

RESTAURANTS I WAITRESSED IN

Stouffer's, in Akron. I was lousy because I had to serve meat to people, which pissed me off. I couldn't be courteous or polite when I wanted to go out and bury the meat like it should have been.

A cocktail bar in Cleveland, When I was twenty three, twenty four

A diner in Kent State. I found it humiliating when guys I fancied came in and I was in my waitress garb, with my hair in a hair net, and I had to serve them. I wouldn't have minded serving them in another capacity.

A snack shop and had to make banana splits. I got fired because this guy kept coming around in a motorcycle and he would rev the engine of the bike and motion for me to come out, which I did.

ONE REASON TO BE VEGETARIAN
Animal slaughter is the beginning and end of all the problems. The human race has become what it is because if someone thinks it's all right to take someone else's life, be it a cat, fly, fish, spider, or whatever, then it's all right to poison the air and water supply,

THE KARMIC REACTION TO WEARING LEATHER
One day you're going to be worn. And all the food you waste in this lifetime you'll go hungry for in the next lifestyle.

MY FAVORITE SOUNDS
The pages of a heavy book being flipped in a library

Footsteps on a street in the dead of night

A BOOK THAT SUMS UP MY PHILOSOPHY
The Bhagavad-Gita. Any question that you have about life can be answered by that book: what you're supposed to do, why you're here, what's going to happen to us, where you were before you were born, and where you're going.

EVENTS I'D LIKE TO HAVE WITNESSED
Jesus driving the merchants out of the temple.

THE MEANING OF THE PILL
It only helps to speed up our demise. It didn't help liberate women, but women' lib started with the pill. What it did is it slowed down's men's liberation—the ones who needed to be liberated. It made men think they could fuck all the time and that it was all right and women just went along with it instead of saying, "No, I don't want to have children, I want to go out and do my thing and have my career, so we're going to have to work this thing out." Instead, people went against the laws of nature, and whenever you go against the laws of nature, ultimately it's destructive. You can't bend those laws, they bend you.

BEST CURES FOR THE BLUES
Heroin—in the immediate sense
Spiritual development—in the permanent sense

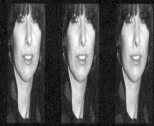

Leonard

MY OLD FLAME

An olive green Olivetti 22 portable typewriter, with black keys and white letters. I bought it in London for forty pounds in 1959. It's the same typewriter I used for my first book and my best works.

WHEN I WRITE

I like the room clean, the floors to be washed, my bed to be made, the table to be tidy. I once had drawn a bath and I put pine oil in it and I noticed the pine oil stained the water the same color as my Olivetti. I was in a mood of some extravagance and I put the typewriter in the bathtub and tried to type under water. Then I threw my manuscript for *Flowers for Hitler* in the bath and tried to scrub it with a nail brush. This was during a particularly tense period one winter in Montreal. Then I took the typewriter out of the bathtub and in a rage over some imagined injustices a woman had done to me, flung it across the room. (It was a small room in a small house I had rented on Pine Avenue.) The Olivetti cracked. I thought it was finished and I just stowed it in a corner of the house. About a year later I went to the Olivetti factory on Nun's Island and brought the thing to the front desk. The man there just looked at it and said "not a chance." Then—I don't know why—when the fellow's back was turned I walked into the factory proper, toward a workbench where an elderly man was working on some typewriters. I approached him and I said I really needed this typewriter. He told me to come back in a few weeks, and when I did he had repaired it meticulously.

A SONG WRITTEN ON THE OLIVETTI

"Suzanne." I met a woman, Mary Martin, who knew me as a Canadian poet and she took me down to New York where I met various people associated with the business and they said, "Stand up, kid. Aren't you a little old for this?" Finally she introduced me to Judy Collins. She was a star then in the circles I respected. A few months later I wrote "Suzanne" and I sang it to her over the phone. She loved it. She recorded it and that gave a certain validity to the work. Then Mary arranged for me to meet John Hammond. He came down to my room at the Chelsea Hotel and he was very sweet. I knew of the people he had brought to Columbia and I was very pleased to be in his company. He said, "What songs do you have?" so I picked up my guitar and sang a song, two songs, five songs, twelve songs, fifteen songs. Then he said he wanted to sign me.

HAD I NOT WRITTEN "SUZANNE"

Presumably I would be broke and starving, as I was then. At thirty-two or thirty-four, whichever I was when I wrote it, I couldn't pay my grocery bills, I couldn't pay the rent, and I had a woman and child to support. Writing that song was a sheer act of desperation—of a desperado.

WHY I WRITE SUCH SAD SONGS

It isn't that I choose to. This is what I am. Seriousness, rather than depression is, I think, the characteristic of my work. I like a good laugh, but I think there's enjoyment that comes through seriousness. We all know when you close the door and come into your room and you're left with your heart and your emotions, it isn't all that funny.

WHY I WRITE THE SAME OLD SONG

I think any artist—writer, singer, or painter—has only one or two paintings that he does over and over.

BIGGEST INFLUENCE ON MY MUSIC

The juke box. I lived beside jukeboxes all through the fifties. There was "The Great Pretender," "Cross Over the Road." I never knew who was singing. I never followed things that way. I still don't. I wasn't a student of music; I was a student of the restaurant I was in—and the waitresses. The music was a part of it. I knew what number the song was.

BIGGEST INFLUENCES ON MY TYPING

Liturgical, country, and folk music. I type very slow at first and work up a head of steam. I type the way I write, one word at a time.

A COUPLE OF PLACES THE OLIVETTI HAS BEEN

New York. In 1966 I borrowed some money from a friend in Montreal and came down to the great empire, America, to try to make my way. I had written a few books and I couldn't make a living. I played in a country band and I loved country music and I had a few songs I thought were country songs and I was on my way ultimately to Nashville but I got ambushed in New York by the folk renaissance—and got my first public appearance at the Newport Folk Festival. In New York I found this huge explosion of things and I was interested in this enlightened community being promoted in the east side of New York and I would go down there but I couldn't locate it. I walked into a club called the Dome and I saw someone singing there who looked like she inhabited a Nazi poster; it was Nico, the perfect Aryan ice queen. And there was a very handsome young man playing for her; he turned out to be Jackson Browne. I just stood there and said forget the new society, this is the

woman I've been looking for. I followed her all around
New York. She led me to Max's Kansas City. I met Lou
Reed there and he said something very kind to me
which made me feel at home. I had no particular clout in
that scene. I was just a guy who was a little older than the
other guys, just sniffing around like everybody else.
I was very lonely and mostly interested in finding a girl.
Lou came over and introduced himself and said, "I love
your book." I never knew anybody knew my books
because they only sold a few thousand copies in America.
We were sitting at a table and some guy was bugging me,
in a polite sort of way, and I was responding in a
polite sort of way, and Lou Reed said to me, "Hey, man,
you don't have to be nice to this guy. You don't have to
be nice to anybody. You're the man who wrote
"Beautiful Losers," Nico eventually told me,
"Look, I like young boys. You're just too old for me."

Hollywood. In 1967 I was invited to score a film. It was
the first time anyone paid my way across the continent and
put me up in a hotel. They even put my name on the
match boxes. Then they showed me the film, but I couldn't
relate to it.

BEST ADVICE MY MOTHER GAVE ME
Before I had gone down to New York—I was already a
grownup man—she said, "Now Leonard, you be careful of
those people, they're not like we are. They're different
from us." I said, "Mother, come on, don't embarrass me by
giving me that kind of advice." I hadn't been living
at home for about sixteen years. I thought it was
very amusing and charming that she said that to me, but it
turned out she was right. Some of the renaissance folk
singers I met pretended to represent my interest and love
my work and eventually pilfered a lot of my work—stole
all my songs—"Suzanne," "Strangers." They tricked me. I
had surrendered half of my publishing on all of the songs
and all of the publishing on all of my hits.

A COUPLE OF PLACES THE OLIVETTI HAS NEVER BEEN
New Mexico. I went alone and checked into a Zen
monastery; there was no time for serious typing. I had met
an eighty-year-old Zen master in L.A. at my friend's
wedding. One of the marriage vows was not to
become intoxicated. Then they broke out the sake, of
which the bride and groom had to drink seven glasses in a

row. A few months later I got into trouble, the kind of trouble that we all embrace but can't name. I went to the Zen master's retreat and stayed the better part of a month. It was too rigorous for me. The master was Japanese and the abbot was German and I'd find myself walking around in the snow wearing sandals at night as part of the walking meditation and thought this was the revenge of the Second World War. They got all these idealistic American kids and were torturing them. I went over the wall, but a couple of things lingered with me and I went back. It's a deep sense of doubt that drives you into the meditation hall, and often it's a self you discover and can't stand, which is why you drop it.

New York. When I went to see Walter Yetnikoff. After reviewing my dark double-breasted suit, Walter said, "Leonard, we know you're great, but we don't know if you're any good," and he turned down *Various Positions* for U.S. distribution because it wasn't contemporary.

HOW I RATE MYSELF
I always considered myself a minor writer. My province is small and I try to explore it very, very thoroughly. It isn't like I chose this. This is what I am. You know whether you're a high jumper or not. I know in a sense I'm a long-distance runner. I'm not going to win any sprints. I'm not going to win any high jumps or anything spectacular. I may hang in there if my health remains good and I will explore this tiny vision.

A SUBJECT I'M OFTEN MISTAKEN TO BE AN EXPERT ON
Love. People in Europe and even here think, because I've written a lot of songs to women, like I was the first guy to do it, I've been pinned with the label of lover, but what they really want me to do is discuss the thing on a level that is deeper or beyond the ordinary realm of the love song, but they aren't. It puts me in the precarious position of being an authority about something that nobody is an authority on. No one masters the heart. That's why we got a million songs about this particular human activity, and in a certain way they're all fresh, whether it's a country-western wine-drinker's song or a Haydn leider about love. That's what we're all interested in. The interest persists because nobody has a real take on it. It's just a matter of longing, holding, and

losing. So to enter into this realm with any sense of authority is inviting humiliation, and quite deservedly so. It's like walking on the stage naked. You got to be in pretty good shape to do that. And it takes a kind of training to speak about these very dangerous kinds of terrain. Unless I really respond authentically to the questions, which would be more or less scratching my head, I don't have any sense of ease about this subject. I don't even know what it means, "a great lover." Is it Casanova? Don Juan? Is it this guy I know who has remarkable success with women, or is it the married man? The monk? I know a man who spent twenty years in a mental hospital because a college love rejected him. Probably the greatest lover I know has never touched a woman, is a virgin at fifty.

WHY I'M NOT A GREAT LOVER
There's something about the description that I find very distasteful and which I would never want applied to me. There's something in it that indicates that the man never loved anybody. Anybody who achieves that title, somehow. I wouldn't want to be on the list. I imagine the guy with the title Great Lover is in the same boat as a guy with the title Poet; he can't get a date.

SOMEONE ELSE WHO CAN'T GET A DATE
Folk singers. Like many other descriptions that once had an aura of glory or honor, such as poet and warrior and priest, folk singers have fallen into complete disgrace. The archetypes are undergoing serious re-evaluation. Folk singers have been in disgrace for so long that some people are actually using it in defiance now, and it has a kind of chic that it didn't have maybe ten years ago. Sometimes I describe myself as a folk singer when I want to present myself as a daring chap. It's much less daring than saying you're a great lover.

WHAT TO TELL A WOMAN AFTER SEX
Thank you.

Faithful

HOW I WAS DISCOVERED

One day after Catholic school, when I was seventeen, I went to a launching party that Andrew Moog Oldham, the Rolling Stones' manager and producer, was throwing for Adrian Poster, a sixteen-year-old singer. It turned out to be my discovery party. It was also the first time I saw Mick Jagger. He was with his girlfriend, Chrissie Shrimpton, the little sister of Jean Shrimpton, the famous fashion model. They had a big fight and I remember being fascinated. I thought it was very grown up, to have a scene like that at a party. But what made that evening was Andrew. He was wonderful. He was a lunatic. He was the whiz kid of his time. Before he was with the Stones he was the Beatles' publicist. That's where he got the idea to produce somebody that was on the opposite side of the coin. He thought up the saying "Would you want your daughter to marry a Rolling Stone?" When he met me he thought I was the perfect foil for them. I looked like an angel, with big tits. He said, "I want to make you a star." It wasn't like Hollywood. It was like London.

WHAT I REMEMBER MOST ABOUT THE '60S

The cover photo of *Sgt. Pepper's*, taken by Michael Cooper. The shot was thought out and discussed endlessly.

Drugs. The intent back then was purer; maybe when the attitude and intention is correct, the effects aren't so bad. But then it all started to go: The Vietnam War got worse, Charlie Manson came along, people started dropping dead from overdoses. It was like an apocalypse.

The Maharishi. I was on that dreadful weekend in Wales with the Beatles, their women, and Mick. I had been living a rather wonderful life with Mick and perhaps for the first time in my life I was experiencing serious emptiness and I needed something other than drugs to fill me up. I was hoping I would get some information. I thought meditation might help and funnily enough it has, but that's years later and it's not the Maharishi. I was on the right track; I was just following the wrong guy.

SONGS THAT CAST THE LONGEST SHADOWS

"As Tears Go By"
"Sister Morphine"
"A Day in the Life"

THE FIRST TIME I SLEPT WITH MICK

I had met Ike and Tina Turner, when they were touring England, at Brian's, and they invited me down to Bristol to catch the show. It was the first time I had seen Ike and Tina; it was also the first time I saw Mick perform. I was backstage, watching Mick watch Tina dance. Then he went out on stage and did it himself. After the show I went to the hotel where the Stones were staying and I smoked more joints than I had ever smoked in my life. Then everybody laid about for hours. Slowly people fell out and I was sitting in a room with Mick and one of the Ikettes. Me and the Ikette were playing a game: who was gong to split first. I hadn't come all the way down to Bristol for nothing. I wanted to see what would happen and who I was going to end up with. Then the Ikette flounced off in a huff, leaving just me and Mick. I got embarrassed and said let's go for a walk; I always found it easier to talk to people when I was walking. We talked about lowlife, Stongehenge, ancient Britain, and King Arthur. I was amazed he knew about those things. I never expected to communicate with him. Then, when we'd had our walk and the sun came up and we'd discussed the Holy Grail, it seemed completely natural to get into bed. It was the beginning of about a year of intense sexual relations. But it wasn't an event. Mick was very nice and cuddly. I would have been scared to death had he been a fantastic demonic lover. I had hoped slightly to find myself in bed with Keith Richards, but I didn't. I found myself in bed with Mick Jagger.

A DREAM I'LL ALWAYS REMEMBER

In 1969, Mick and I flew to Australia to make *Ned Kelly* with Tony Richardson. As soon as we got off the plane, we had a very nasty reception. About a hundred Australian reporters were down on the tarmac freaking out because Mick Jagger was going to play their folk hero. In those days, Australia was like Britain in the 1950s, when I grew up. They were incredibly puritanical and this faggot coming to play their big macho hero was the greatest insult. New line I was pretty much gone by the time the plane landed. I was frightened of flying, or so I said. That was my excuse. I would go to the doctor and say, "I got a long flight and I need some downers." On this occasion I said, "and I'll be away for three months." The doctor gave me a prescription to last three months. I must have taken fifteen Tuinals during the flight. By the time we got to the hotel, I was in a trance. When we got to our room, Mick went straight to sleep. I decided to take the rest of the pills. But first I walked around a bit and had a few visions. I just didn't take a limo to the hotel, check into my room, and try to kill myself. What frightened me terribly was that we were high up in a hotel room and I couldn't open the windows. Had a window been open, I think I would have jumped. I saw things down on the street that couldn't have been there. I saw Brian Jones, who had just died from an apparent drug overdose five days before. The moment I thought I saw him I went into a coma that lasted six days.

The central vision went on for a long time. I had gone onto the other side. There was no weather, no wind or rain or sunshine or darkness. There was nothing at all.

The place looked like the illustrations in books by Edmond Du Lac and those Durer engravings of hell. I was very interested in opiate literature at the time and this vision was definitely on an opiate scale. The grandeur and enormity of the place and the general feeling was like one of those engravings. But surroundings didn't interest me as much as walking along with Brian, who had woken up dead and didn't know where he was. Lots of people do that. We walked along and talked and talked. It was the nicest chat I ever had with him. We talked about everything you could imagine: how he had woken up not knowing where he was and put out his hand for his Valium or his drugs and there was nothing and how frightened he was. He was lonely and confused and brought me to the other side to walk with him on this particular bit of the journey, which I did with pleasure. Afterwards he said he was very sorry to have put me in this fix. I didn't mind; I understood how he felt. He didn't know he was dead. I'm sure when people die quickly, they must go through terrible confusion. They don't know that they're dead. That's why there are ghosts. Ghosts are people who don't quite realize they are dead. Death is the next great adventure. That's what Brian and I talked about.

Then, when we got to the end of the Du Lac or Durer vision, the edge over which you went or not, Brian slipped off and I didn't. I heard voices calling me back, but I still had some more adventures to go on along the way. Getting back took a long time. It was like jogging through a place that was very monochromatic, like a ghost town where there were other people jogging or floating along. Or an *Alice in Wonderland* dream, where the feet don't quite touch the ground. I dreamed I was lost in an airport and people were coming up to me asking, "Where are you going?" "What are you doing here?" And I would say, "I'm waiting for Mick to come and get me,"

and he did. If he hadn't woken up and got me to the hospital so quickly, I would have slipped over the edge with Brian. Six days later I woke up in a hospital and when I opened my eyes I saw my mother and Mick. I think my mother was by my side in the hospital all the time. I think Mick wasn't. He was drumming back and forth from his work. Nothing stops Mick when he's working, not even an attempted suicide. He's got to be ultraprofessional; wouldn't expect different. If Mick tried to kill himself while I was working, I wouldn't stop either.

I felt very bad about what I did. I must have caused a tremendous amount of trouble. I've always taken my anger out on myself. People who commit suicide are usually doing it to punish someone else for something. It's a weapon to make people feel bad. I was obviously punishing Mick because Brian Jones had just died, and I was angry about the way he and Keith treated him. Brian was a hopeless mess and they were just so cool. Brian really fucked himself up by letting himself get much, much, much too involved in drugs, even before Keith got like that. I always felt Keith's way of reacting to Brian's death was to become Brian. But Keith is so strong physically that he didn't look like he was disintegrating. Brian really did disintegrate.

THE MOST FAMOUS RUMOR ABOUT ME

That the Rolling Stones ate a Mars bar out of my vagina the night of Mick's drug bust. What happened was Mick, Keith, I and a bunch of friends went down to West Wittering, where Keith had a house, and took LSD. The trip was planned around going to a house owned by a great surrealist art collector, but it was Sunday and the place was closed. We spent our LSD trip in a Land Rover, which wasn't very pleasant. When we got back to Keith's, the first thing I did was have a bath. When I got out of the bath I realized I hadn't brought anything to change into. The only thing I could see myself wearing was a beautiful fur rug, which was in the bedroom. So I put on the rug and without anything on underneath, came down to the drawing room, sat on the couch, watched the fire, and smoked a joint.
Then about twenty five cops busted in.
I thought it was a joke. At about that time the Rolling

Stones were getting dangerous, or so the establishment thought, and had to be taken down a peg or two, and the *News of the World* somehow got our phones tapped, found out we were going down to West Wittering to take LSD, and decided to bust Mick Jagger. They only got four little uppers on Mick which were mine; they didn't get the LSD. As for me, I just sat there in my fur rug, with no Mars bar, but for some reason people want to believe that when the cops walked in there was this incredible orgy going on.

MY EARLIEST ROLE MODELS

The sickest ones I could find. Usually they were dead and black, like Billie Holiday, Ma Rainey, Memphis Minnie. Now they're not terrifying anymore. I see them as dead, black, and friendly.

A COUPLE OF LEGENDS WHO ARE TRULY LEGENDARY

Jimi Hendrix. He had amazing sexual power. Legends always have that erotic power. I happened to go to his first show, in some dive in London. I was nineteen and literally the only person in the audience. It was just me, Jimi, the Experience, the roadies, and the waitresses. I felt I had discovered him.

Madonna. She was really done up and looked great. I went to her house and saw all her paintings. Then we went to the theater and then dancing. She acted like Madonna. I could never do that when I meet people. I always manage to say something inappropriate and not very Marianne Faithful-like. When I met Madonna, I managed to get through the whole evening without saying much at all. She behaved like her and I behaved like me.

SOMEONE I'M SURPRISED IS STILL ALIVE

Captain Beefheart. I'm pleased that he's still around. I
never thought he'd make it. It's not only drugs that kill
you. He's very sensitive, and you can die from that.

A PHOTOGRAPHS THAT ONCE SUMMED ME UP

The one David Bailey took of me when I was seventeen for
British *Vogue*. Nearly every picture in British *Vogue* at the
time (1964) was Bailey. It was taken on
Primrose Hill. You see the hill at an angle with a man
sitting on a bench in the distance. I'm sitting in the grass. It
took all day to get this picture, and by the time we got it, it
was night. Of course it was in black and white. The sky's
very black and the trees are very black and
there are clouds. It's very gothic. My least favorite
photograph, but one that captured me at the time, was
taken of me in the hospital while I was still unconscious
from a drug overdose. Somehow a newspaper
photographer got into the intensive care ward and with
the aid of a flashlight, took a picture of me lying with all
these tubes stuck into my face.

A PHOTOGRAPH THAT BEST SUMS ME UP NOW

I'm at home in my five-sided room of an
eighteenth-century cottage in Ireland. I'm sitting
cross-legged in this beautiful chair covered in colorful
Hungarian embroidered material. There's a
three-thousand-year-old elk's head hanging on the wall
behind me and I'm looking out a
gothic window at a lake with swans and herons.
I'm completely isolated and
protected, with two gates between me and the world.

Jackson Browne

EARLY ROLE MODELS

The *chollos*—guys from the neighborhood. It was a Chicano thing, the way they dressed: khakis, French toe shoes, white T-shirts, Sir Guy shirts—a dress shirt with pleats in the back that you'd iron so they almost formed a wing, like the fins of a '59 Impala. The Chicanos, where I grew up in the Highland Park section of Los Angeles, dressed immaculately, always pressed. Everybody grew up ironing. They combed their hair straight back, with a big wave in front and a duck's ass in back. And they drove '32 coupes with chopped roofs. The white guys from Eagle Rock, those who had money, wore new blue jeans, white T-shirts, and tennis shoes and drove white '59 Impalas.

MAJOR OUTFITS FROM MY WARDROBE

The yellow checked shirt and grey slacks my mother bought me when I was a little kid, to be on the Art Linkletter show

The Sir Guy shirt I wore when I was eleven or twelve

A tan corduroy jacket with brown leather buttons—it was a family tradition that when they're sixteen everybody get their picture taken at the house I grew up in that my grandfather built, and this is what I wore. It's the same jacket I wore the first time I took acid and was exulting over the fact that every time I put my hand into the lining and rummaged around, I'd pull out a different combination of burnt match, ball of lint and fortune cookie.

Stussy—now what I wear is influenced by my kids; because you got to take them to get clothes, you suddenly find a bunch of this stuff on yourself.

WHAT I'D WEAR TO BE PHOTOGRAPHED IN FRONT OF MY GRANDFATHER'S HOUSE NOW

A black Paul Smith suit with a white shirt and black shoes. I dress in a combination of Amish and California skate.

A POSSESSION THAT'S BEEN A SILENT WITNESS TO MY LIFE

A drawing by Paul Gaugin of his child-bride lying on a bed in Tahiti. He was warned never to leave her alone at night and he did accidentally on this one occasion and when he came back she was almost in a trance and in a spooky state. I took this drawing out of a book years ago and it's been on my nightstand since.

SOME MORE THINGS ON MY NIGHTSTAND

A little clock
A post card from a friend in Hawaii
A letter from my girlfriend
An empty bottle of beer
A cloisonné lamp that I've had for close to twenty years
A photograph I recently found of my fourth grade class, when I was a cub scout

THE LAST JOB I HAD THAT I NEEDED AN ALARM CLOCK FOR

Assembling kaleidoscopes at the California Kaleidoscope factory when I was eighteen or so. If one more person came up and said, "oooh, oooh, oooh, look at that!" I would have lost my mind. I lasted a week.

THE FIRST EXTRAVAGANT THING I BOUGHT

Probably guitars—but I was buying guitars before then, so it wasn't so dramatic. I came from a period in time that wasn't geared to accumulating a stash of great stuff, because you were just as likely to give it away as keep it. I mean, I got one car that's my car, that I drive and take care of.

MY FAVROITE DRIVE

L.A. to Colorado—you go through the California desert on Highway 40, across the Arizona desert, past Hopi and Navajo, into New Mexico. You see this incredible, curving, low terrain that swoops up to the mountains in the distance. As the miles go by, you sort of empty out. You might not speak for a hundred miles, then have a conversation that's from the center of your life.

CAR I DRIVE

A 1969 Chevrolet Malibu convertible

SONGS THAT CAME TO ME WHILE DRIVING

"Take It Easy" was written on a trip like that; "Running On Empty" wasn't—that came out of a sound check. The same thing happens when touring with six or seven people who share the inside of a bus for months at a time. There's the repetition of the routine: getting on the bus and going some place, getting off the bus and doing a show. It's almost meditative, especially if you're in the company of people you really like and trust, which is what you try to make happen when you put together a band. It's almost as important a consideration as how well they play.

PEOPLE I'D MOST LIKE TO RIDE ON A BUS WITH

Jack Kerouac
Neil Cassidy
Allen Ginsberg
Chief Joseph and the Nez Perce
Dylan and the Hawks—the early Band
I would like to have driven them into Canada and helped them allude the U.S. Army

SOMEONE I'VE SPENT A LOT OF TIME THINKING ABOUT

Dylan—There are probably very few people I've thought as much about in my life—if you were logging the hours. But I never thought it was necessary to get to know him. Maybe that's the ultimate form of hero worship. I took him at his word when he'd say things like, "I don't know why anybody would want to know me, it would be just like knowing you." He's one of the stranger people. When I met him at one of my concerts, he didn't move a muscle. It was indoors but he had on this fur cap and shades and gloves. It was a little like meeting an icon or a statue; maybe like meeting one of those Easter Island statues. It kind of wigged me out because I had just gotten through singing. Somebody had said he was in the audience, so I thought about it the entire time I was singing. In the middle I thought I saw someone stand up and leave, so I relaxed and finished my set. Then, when I started to leave, the club owner pulled me into a booth and introduced me to Bob Dylan and my mind was blown all over again.

SONGS THAT HAVE SERVED AS LANDMARKS

"Love You So," by Ron Holden—
one of the earliest songs I can remember.
"Maybe," by the Chantels
"Stay With Me Baby," by Lorraine Ellison
"Everyday People"
"Walk Away Rene"
A lot of early Dylan
When music moves you, your psyche becomes implanted
with the time and the place, like a little stamp.
Sometimes you're reminded of things you haven't thought
of for a long time, that you might have forgotten. There are
all sorts of things we don't want to remember
or don't allow ourselves to remember or can't remember
except under certain conditions.

SONGS THAT WILL ALWAYS REMIND ME OF DARYL HANNAH

Some of the songs on *I'm Alive*—they were written during
the last four years, during which we were together
and breaking up and not together. But to say these songs
are about one specific person sort of defeats their purpose.
I don't think I want to talk about my personal

relationships on that level. It's too hard to have any privacy
in the first place. A relationship is a very private
thing. Unfortunately it can become very public, but the real
truth of it is very private and is something to be protected;
not something to be discussed casually and openly.
And I've never been the object of that kind of attention. It's
like getting hit by a car while crossing the street. It
becomes the most widely known thing about a person, by
people who don't know me.

DID I GIVE DARYL HANNAH A BLACK EYE?

Absolutely not. It really is hard to see shit printed and let it
go by and I chose to do that. I think my work speaks
for itself and what I'm about and what is inside of me is in
my records. I deal with it in that way. *I'm Alive* is
not meant to be a document or an account, but it does
represent my interior.

HOW A LIFE EXPERIENCE BECOMES A SONG

The example I have in mind is "In the Shape of a Heart."
It's amazing what happens to me when I sing this song. I
wrote it about my wife committing suicide in the 1970s. But

179

it doesn't have to be about her; it could be about anybody who you lost, about any relationship that didn't quite make it. And even though it's partially about the futility that arises out of not having words that really adequately describe these things, I do happen to like the lyrics. They valiantly attempt to say these things. It's in the attempt that there's some grace or beauty.

HOW I'D DESCRIBE THE CALIFORNIA ROCK SCENE OF THE '70S

I resist all the descriptions of the '70s, just like you have to resist descriptions of the '60s—there were a lot of different '60s going on at the same time. Most people, when talking about the '60s, are talking about this amazing period with all these possibilities, all this promise, all this mind-expansion, all kinds of drugs and sexual freedom. But it was a real tumultuous time, with all sorts of tumultuous political happenings that formed all of our lives, whether we were political or not. I think that process kept happening in the '70s. It was the other side of the cycle, where people had to realize that it wasn't as easy as having these dreams, that you have to make the dreams work. It was kind of what *The Pretender* was about—the idea of investing in the material life and putting the ideal life on hold.

HOW A SENSITIVE SONGWRITER SURVIVED THE '70S

I don't think I'm that sensitive; it's more that I'm supposed to be. I mean, sensitivity is a good thing, but the professional sensitive person is ludicrous. Everybody's sensitive—to certain things. I got through the seventies by taking a lot of drugs.

HOW I MANAGED TO COME OUT INTACT, WHILE SO MANY OF MY PEERS DIDN'T

Well, I can look at my own life and assay the damage that drugs took. But early on I became associated with a number of people who were involved in the environment and human rights. I was really inspired by them because to me it was the embodiment of the ideas of the sixties. And the other thing that got me through the seventies, the most obvious thing, was having the responsibility of bringing up a kid.

HOW RELATIONSHIPS BETWEEN MEN AND WOMEN HAVE CHANGED SINCE THE '70S

They haven't. Some things never change. It's possible to learn a great deal in a relationship and it's possible to forget everything you know and have to learn it again. I'm forty-five and I have a kid who's twenty. I don't think in terms of '70s or '90s. I think in terms of being twenty or forty-five. Relationships have to do with bringing up kids and becoming a parent. When bringing up kids, you have a lot of time to reflect on how you were brought up. There's a paradox: You have to be there for them and provide some structure, but at the same time we all know that you can only learn stuff by doing it yourself. There comes a time when a kid rejects everything you taught him just so he can go off and be his own person. Hopefully at some point you get back together.

THE HARDEST PART ABOUT BEING A PARENT TODAY

It's an impossible situation, bringing up kids in an environment that's so dangerous. And it's terrible if you're trying to advocate certain kinds of behavior that you didn't have to observe yourself. Sexual abstinence? Come on. Abstinence from drugs? And of course kids have a bullshit detector. They are allergic to hypocrisy—and oblivious to their own.

HOW LOVE HAS CHANGED

It hasn't, it's just been employed to sell so many cars, so much perfume, and so many jeans, that people have been inoculated against it, but the reason it works in advertising is because it's so strong. There's that saying, "Hope spring eternal." Love is a sacred thing. It's what makes life livable.

Queen Latifa

THREE TEEN IDOLS
Patti LaBelle. She had a beautiful voice and an exciting presence.
Tina Marie. She had a fabulous voice and a fabulous presence.
Elton John

THREE CURRENT IDOLS
Patti LaBelle
Tina Marie
Anita Baker

SOME DISHES THAT INFLUENCED MY MUSIC
Curried chicken
Chili
Chocolate ice cream

A CROWD IN HISTORY I WISH I HAD BEEN IN
The one at the Diana Ross concert in Central Park when she fell on stage

A COUPLE OF SONGS THAT GET ME HOT
"Adore"
and "Scandalous," by Prince

MY FAVORITE POET
Susan Polis Schutz. She writes those really deep things on greeting cards.

AT THE TOP OF MY SHOPPING LIST
An audio system for my car
An alarm for my car
Seat covers
A tint on my windows

IF I WERE A MAN
I'd like to be Denzel Washington.

THE NEAREST FARAWAY PLACE
Eagle Rock Reservation, New Jersey

THE BEST CURE FOR THE BLUES
Chili

Neil Young

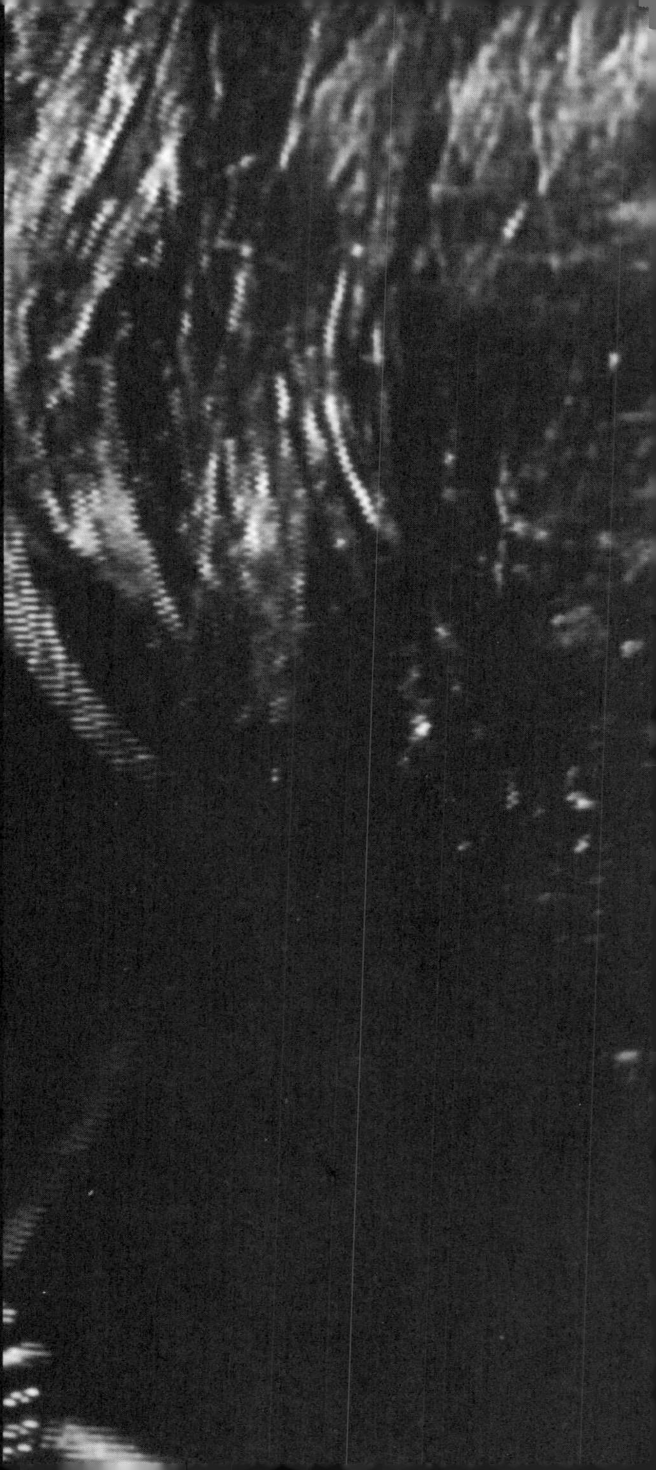

RECORDS THAT HAVE INFLUENCED MY SONGS
"Are You Experienced," by Jimi Hendrix
A Bert Jansch that was available only in Canada
Some early Beatles records
And when I was really into music as a young teenager:
Ronnie Self
The Bobettes
The Chantels
The Fireballs.

WHEN I WAS A TEEN, PEOPLE WHO WERE ON MY BEST-DRESSED LIST
Me. I was way ahead of the styles. Actually, I was a
couple of years behind, but it was unique the
way I stayed behind all the time. I was wearing what
everyone had been wearing two years earlier. Like white
bucks. I had some two years after they
went out of style. That's what made me write the
songs and play the guitar;
because I was so cool in my white bucks. What
I like now is a T-shirt, jeans, and
dirty white bucks.

BANDS I WOULD LIKE TO HAVE WATCHED WORK
Link Wray and the Wraymen
Buddy Holly and the Crickets
Lonnie Mack doing "Wham" and "Memphis"
Jimmy Reed
Hound Dog Taylor
The early Rolling Stones, a year before they recorded. I'd
just like to have seen how these bands looked,
the techniques they were using, and how it felt to be there
while they were playing.

RECORDS I WISH I HAD NEVER LOST
The Early Shadows, from England

My old Jimmy Reed collection

Larry Williams—"Bony Moronie," and all of those original
78s, when they first came out

My 45s collection—especially "Little Star," by the
Elements and "Book of Love," by the Monotones

Very early Everly Brothers

A DEPARTMENT STORE WINDOW I'D LIKE TO DRESS

One in New York, Chicago, or maybe Harrod's in London. It would have to be a fucking long store, a whole block, where they had a series of windows. I'd do a horticultural sculpture with a complete life cycle made to look like miniatures: burned-out stumps that look like mountains, grassy hills that were actually just moss, and rivers and lakes with wildlife living in them. Every window would have a different climate and terrain, with a train layout running throughout the whole thing, as if the train were going across America.

PHOTOGRAPHS I WISH I HAD BEEN IN

The camera hadn't been invented yet, but I wish I could have been photographed looking into the camera with the Egyptians behind me building the pyramids. I wish I could have been in South America while they were building the pyramids there. That way, besides me looking cool, you'd see in the background how the pyramids were built.

ACTORS I'D SEE ANY MOVIE THEY WERE IN

Dennis Hopper and Danny Aiello

AN ACTOR I WANT TO PLAY ME IN MY LIFE STORY

Tom Cruise

THE FIRST EXPENSIVE THING I BOUGHT WITH MY FIRST BIG PAYCHECK

When I was twenty I bought a big redwood house on a hillside in Topanga Canyon. It was pretty good until our car slipped out of the garage one night, went straight down the hill, knocked into the support pillars of a neighbor's house, and the house fell down.

THE RIVER WHERE I SHOT MY BABY

The same river that shows up in "Broken Arrow" and "Powerfinger"

SOME SONGS THAT MOST OF MY OTHER SONGS ARE VARIATIONS OF

"The Loner," which was the first of several songs that developed into several others down the line, like "Cinnamon Girl," "Cowgirl in the Sand," "Like a Hurricane,"

and "Fucking Up." Country-flavored songs like "The Losing End," "Field of Opportunity," and "Comes a Time" keep recurring. Pounding rockers like "Rust Never Sleeps" —these are like my footsteps; it's not so much a technique as an atmosphere.

THE SONG THAT IS MOST ME

"Will to Love." That one was out there. That was one of my best pieces because there was nothing about it that wasn't me. I played everything on it, wrote it, recorded it on a cassette recorder in front of a fireplace, then transferred it to multi-track and added only the shading of instruments where I heard them and didn't play them when I didn't hear them, so instruments come and go throughout the song seemingly at random. That was a true, uninterrupted expression that came from deep inside.

WHEN I WAS YOUNG AND ON MY OWN, HOW IT FELT TO BE ALL ALONE

A recurring feeling. It happened when the seasons changed. It was almost like a plant. The seasons'll change and the leaves'll be blowing, and I'd get this feeling over my whole body; then months would go by and I'd feel it again, but I don't know what the fuck it is. Now I'm older and it doesn't seem to happen anymore; maybe once in a while—I might take a walk down to the lake and just look around and I feel it, but it's not like it was. It's like the shine's not on it.

A LINE THAT KEEPS COMING BACK TO ME

"How does it feel?"

HOW TO BE SURE RIGHT FROM THE START

The fuck if I know. If you're going to do something like get married, you got to try to be sure, because you're making a commitment, and you might have children, and then you better have your shit together. And we've all—well, a number of us—have thought we had it together and didn't, and had to start over again.

HOW TO MAKE ARRANGEMENTS WITH YOURSELF WHEN YOU'RE OLD ENOUGH TO REPAY BUT YOUNG ENOUGH TO SELL

That's a hell of a question, isn't it? I don't understand it. It sounds like gibberish to me. I stopped singing that song because when I get to that line I go, what the fuck am I talking about? I don't edit my songs. I knew something was happening at the time that I wrote it to make that right, but I can't remember what.

"I Am a Child" is also like that. "Now that you made yourself love me, do you think I can change it in a day?" That's a heavy one. That song has the most haunting lyrics. "Am I lying to you when I say I believe in you?"; that song I can hardly talk about. That one is deep. I think I only sang it live two or three times, and only in the studio two or three times, so I may have only sung that song six times total.

WHEN I DANCE

My senses tingle and I take a chance—but I have to have a few drinks first.

THE DIFFERENCE BETWEEN REDWOOD AND HOLLYWOOD

Redwood is a good place to get away from Hollywood.

WHERE I FOUND A HEART OF GOLD

In my little girl and in my wife.

WHAT MY HEART IS MADE OF

I think something shines in there sometimes, but I don't know what it is. It could be fool's gold, but I don't think so. It's not brass. It's light. But not Bud Lite.

THE WOMAN INSIDE ME WHO WANTS ME TO PLAY THE GAME

She's probably good looking. She might be a twin. That's why there's bisexualism and homosexualism; there's no separating these people. I think there's women inside all of us and men inside all of the women.

A WOMAN I'D MOST LIKE TO BE

Eve

WHY I'D RATHER BURN OUT THAN RUST

Rust implies you're not using anything, that you're sitting there letting the elements eat you.

Burning up means you're cruising through the elements so fucking fast that you're actually burning, and your circuits, instead of corroding, are fucking disintegrating.

You're going so fast you're actually fucking the elements, becoming one with the elements, turning to gas.

THINGS A MAN NEEDS

A key ring, with the possibility of having a lot of keys and to be able to take them off and throw them away

Room service

A good breeze every once in a while

Eventually, at some time in his life, a man really needs a good brass band.

ONE THING THAT CAN BREAK MY HEART

Love, that's about it.

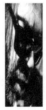

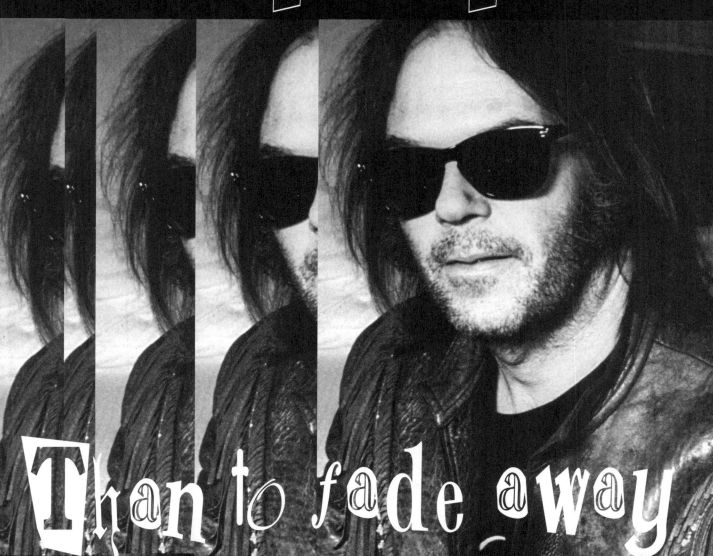

It's better to burn out

Than to fade away

Acknowledgments

Special thanks to
Sandy Choron, Dave Dunton, Paul Leibow,
Jim Thiel, Sharon Mendelow, Casey Choron, Jake Guralnick, Victor Weaver,
and the editors, photographers, and publicists for their kind help.

About The Author

SCOTT COHEN was one of the original editors of *Spin,* and former sports editor of *Interview.* His works
have appeared in the "Style" section of *The New York Times, Details, Elle, Allure,* and
Playboy, and numerous other magazines. He is the author of three books: *Meet Your Maker; Jocks;* and
Zap: The Rise and Fall of Atari.

Many of the interviews in this book have appeared in a related form in
Spin, Details, Egg, and *Circus.*

Photo Credits

ARTIST	PHOTOGRAPHER	ARTIST	PHOTOGRAPHER
Bob Dylan, pp.10,17	Charlyn Zlotnik/L.F.I.	Ice-T, pp.74,77	The Douglas Brothers/ONYX
Bob Dylan, p.12	Ilpo Musto/L.F.I.	Ice-T, Darlene, two dogs, p.76	Guzman
Bob Dylan, p.14,19	L.F.I. © (London Features Int.)	Ice-T, p.78	Jesse Frohman/L.F.I.
Patti Smith, p.20,27	David Gahr	Iggy Pop, p.80,87	Mick Rock
Patti Smith, pp.22,23	Raeanne Rubenstein	Iggy Pop, p.82	Andy Catlin/L.F.I.
Patti Smith, p.25	Photo By David Godlis	Iggy Pop, p.83,84	Roberta Bayley
Red Hot Chili Peppers, pp.28-29	Gavin Bowden	Iggy Pop, p.85	Claude Van Heye/L.F.I.
Screamin' Jay Hawkins, pp.31,33	Masayoshi Sukita	Salt'N'Pepa, pp.88,89,90,93	Andy Catlin/L.F.I.
Lenny Kravitz, pp.34,36	L.F.I. © (London Features Int.)	Salt 'N' Pepa, p.92	Phil Loftus/L.F.I.
Lenny Kravitz, p.36	D. Ridgers/L.F.I.	Salt 'N' Pepa, p.91	Phil Nicholls/L.F.I.
David Bowie, pp.37,38,39,40	Mick Rock	David Lee Roth, p.96,97	Ross Marino/L.F.I.
David Bowie, p.41	K. Vraa/L.F.I.	David Lee Roth, p.98	Jim Hagopian
Tina Turner, p.42	Joe Bangay/L.F.I.	David Lee Roth, p.99	Paul Canty/L.F.I.
Tina Turner, pp.44,45	Peter Ashworth/L.F.I.	James Brown, p.100	Robin Kaplan/L.F.I.
Tina Turner,Ikettes, p.46	L.F.I. © (London Features Int.)	James Brown, p.101	Buster Browne/L.F.I.
Tina Turner, p.47	L.F.I. © (London Features Int.)	James Brown, p.102	Eugene Adebari/L.F.I.
Jonathan Richman &		Young M.C., p.104,105	The Douglas Brothers/ONYX
The Modern Lovers, pp.48-49	Richard Rodgers, courtesy	Bryan Ferry, p.106	Peter Ashworth/L.F.I.
	Ernie Brooks	Bryan Ferry, p.107	Phil Loftus/L.F.I.
Jonathan Richman, p.51	Thomas Consilvio	Bryan Ferry & Anna Nicole Smith,	
Jonathan Richman &		p.108	L. Lawry/L.F.I.
The Modern Lovers, p.52	Thomas Consilvio	Bryan Ferry, p.109	Peter Mazel/L.F.I.
Bobby Brown, p.56	Ron Wolfson/L.F.I.	Bryan Ferry, p.109	Tom Sheehan/L.F.I.
Bobby Brown, p.57	Aubrey Reuben/L.F.I.	RuPaul, pp.110,112,113	Joe Major/L.F.I.
Captain Beefheart, p.58	L.F.I. © (London Features Int.)	Laurie Anderson, p.114	Anastasia Pantsios/L.F.I.
Captain Beefheart, p.59	Mick Rock	Laurie Anderson, p.115	Russell Young/L.F.I.
Madonna, p.60,61	Melodie McDaniel/L.F.I.	Laurie Anderson, p.116	Gilles Larrain/L.F.I.
Madonna, p.62	Mark D/L.F.I.	Brian Wilson, p.117	Kamron Hinatsu/L.F.I.
Madonna, pp.62,63	Herb Ritts	Beach Boys, p.120	Raeanne Rubenstein
Al Green, p.64	Ron Wolfson/L.F.I.	Brian Wilson, p.121	Raeanne Rubenstein
David Byrne, pp.66,67	Nick Elgar/L.F.I.	Brian Wilson,p.123	Ron Wolfson/L.F.I.
David Byrne, p.68	Photo By David Godlis	Run, p.124	Kristin Callahan/L.F.I.
David Byrne, p.69	Bonnie Schiffman/L.F.I.	Run D.M.C., pp.124-125	George DuBose/L.F.I.
Malcolm McLaren, p.70	Nick Egan, Keith Haring	Run D.M.C., p126-127	Ilpo Musto/L.F.I.
Malcolm McLaren, p.72	N. Vinieratos/L.F.I.	Steven Tyler, p.128	L.F.I. © (London Features Int.)

ARTIST	PHOTOGRAPHER
Steven Tyler, p.129	G. Kirkland/L.F.I.
Steven Tyler, p.131	Ross Marino/L.F.I.
Aretha Franklin,p.132	Courtesy Sony Music
Aretha Franklin, p.134	Courtesy Sony Music
Duran Duran, p.135	George DuBose/L.F.I.
John Taylor, p.136	Phil Loftus/L.F.I.
John Taylor, p.137	Simon Fowler/L.F.I.
Nick Rhodes, p.138	Simon Fowler/L.F.I.
Nick Rhodes, p.139	Lawrence Lawry/L.F.I.
Simon LeBon, pp.141,143	Paul Cox/L.F.I.
Simon LeBon, p.142	Joe Bangay/PIX INT'L
Big Daddy Kane, p.144	Marcus Morianz/L.F.I.
Big Daddy Kane, p.145	George DuBose/L.F.I.
Big Daddy Kane, p.145	The Douglas Brothers/ONYX
John Cale, p.146	Deborah Feingold/L.F.I.
Lou Reed, p.148	Derek Ridgers/L.F.I.
Andy Warhol, p.148	Raeanne Rubenstein
John Cale, p.149	Paul Cox/L.F.I.
John Cale, Lou Reed, p.150	W. Abbott/L.F.I.
Lou Reed, p.152	Diego Uchitel/L.F.I.
Reed,Cale,Warhol, p.154	UWA/L.F.I.
Lou Reed, p.155 (both)	Mick Rock
Chrissie Hynde, p.156,157	Simon Fowler/L.F.I.
Chrissie Hynde, p.158	L.F.I. © (London Features Int.)
Chrissie Hynde, p.159	Jill Furmanovsky/L.F.I.
Chrissie Hynde, p.160	Ilpo Musto/L.F.I.
Leonard Cohen, p.162	Clouds Studios/L.F.I.
Leonard Cohen, p.164	Raeanne Rubenstein
Leonard Cohen, p.165	Lawry/L.F.I.
Leonard Cohen, p.166	Raeanne Rubenstein
Chrissie Hynde, p.161	Ilpo Musto/L.F.I.
Marianne Faithfull, pp.168,170	L.F.I. © (London Features Int.)
Mick Jagger, p.171	L.F.I. © (London Features Int.)
Marianne Faithfull, pp.172,175	Adrian Boot/L.F.I.
Rolling Stones, p.173	L.F.I. © (London Features Int.)
Mick & Brian, p.174	L.F.I. © (London Features Int.)
Jackson Browne, p.176	John Garone/L.F.I.
Jackson Browne, p.177,180	Gregg De Guire/L.F.I.
Jackson Browne & Darryl Hannah, p.179	R.J. Capak/L.F.I.

ARTIST	PHOTOGRAPHER
Jackson Browne, p.181	Geoff Swaine/L.F.I.
Queen Latifah, pp.182,183	The Douglas Brothers/ONYX
Neil Young, p.184,185	Still taken from video by
	Joel Bernstein
Neil Young, p.186	L.F.I. (c) London Features Int.
Neil Young, p.186	R.J. Capak/L.F.I.
Neil Young, p.189	Paul Sheehan/L.F.I.

Every attempt has been made to properly credit the photographers. In the event of an omission or error, please contact the Publishers, and any corrections will be made to the subsequent printings of this book.